CW01521585

Dream Catcher 37

Stairwell Books //

Dream Catcher 37

Editor Emeritus
And Founder
Paul Sutherland

Editor
John Gilham

Editorial Board
John Gilham
Tanya Parker Nightingale
Pauline Kirk
Eleanor Higginson
Rose Drew
Alan Gillott
Greg McGee

Art Advisor
Greg McGee

Reviews Editor
Tanya Parker Nightingale

Production Managers
Alan Gillott and Rose Drew

SUBSCRIPTIONS TO
DREAM CATCHER
MAGAZINE

£15.00 UK (Two issues inc. p&p)
£22.00 Europe
£25.00 USA and Canada

Cheques should be made
payable to **Dream Catcher**
and sent to:

Dream Catcher Subscriptions
161 Lowther Street
York, YO31 7LZ
UK

+44 1904 733767

argillott@gmail.com

www.dreamcatchermagazine.co.uk
@literaryartsmag
www.stairwellbooks.co.uk
@stairwellbooks

Dream Catcher Magazine

Dream Catcher No. 37

© Alan Smith, Ali Pardoe, Alice Harrison, Alice West, Alison Mordey, Angela Cooke, Angelica Krikler, Ann Heath, Becca Miles, Ben Benison, C M Buckland, Cedric Pickin, Charles Douglas, Charlotte McCormac, Claire Booker, Clint Wastling, Clive Donovan, Damon Young, Daniel Gustafsson, David J. Costello, Diana Cant, Diana Powell, Donna Williams, Eleanor Porter, Elisabeth Jeffreys, Freya Horsley, Gay McKenna, Glen Proctor, Grahaeme Barrasford Young, Helen Parker, Iain Twiddy, Imogen Godwin, Jacqueline Sousa, James B. Nicola, Jamie Lynch, Jane Stuart, John Gilham, John Vale, Josephine von Zitzewitz, Kathleen McPhilemy, Ken Gambles, Kenneth Durham Smith, Kieran Egan, Linda Lee Welch, Linda Rose Parkes, Lizzie Holden, Merryn Williams, Michael Newman, Mike McNamara, Mike O'Brien, Miranda Day, Natalie Scott, Ness Al-Shaikhly, Nick Boreham, Oleg Okhapkin, Oz Hardwick, Patricia Leighton, Paul Brownsey, Peter J King, Phil Connolly, Ray Malone, Sally Festing, Scott Butterworth, Stewart J. Lowe, Susan Wallace, Tanvir Ratul, Tanya Parker Nightingale, Thelma Laycock, Tom Vaughan, Tony McCabe, Yvonne Hendrie,
2018

The moral rights of authors and artists have been asserted

ISSN: 1466-9455

Published by Stairwell Books //

ISBN: 978-1-939269-80-5

York UNESCO
City of Media Arts

Contents – Authors

FEATURED ARTIST

Led by her responses to landscape, light and weather and also by the process of painting itself, Freya creates paintings that refer to both the permanent elemental nature of land and a more ephemeral sense of fluidity and change. In drawings made on the spot and in larger paintings in her studio, Freya captures the intangibility of the changes which rain, mist, sunlight, cloud, snow bring to the face of the land. There is a Turnerian harnessing of light and how it sculpts new textures as it changes. Collectors have remarked that it is not simply the balmy calming qualities inherent in her output, but it is this, the relentless homage to light, reminiscent of the Romantic painters and their highly attuned attachment to nature, that attracts them and has made for such successful exhibitions. Perhaps in these days of breakneck capitalism and its adverts, Google cookies, and harvested personal data, echoes of the Romantics are just what we need to bring some much needed meaning to our visual culture.

Freya is increasingly keen to explore in greater depth the relationship between what is being painted and how it comes about; how much is real place and how much painted space. Drawing and making notes outside in the landscape allows her to instill in her mind a feeling of a place with its sights and sounds. However, the separation involved in making the paintings back in the studio is equally important to how Freya approaches her work freely, as a painting rather than as a detailed geographical record.

It is this second aspect, the controlled chronicling in the studio, which has been sparking the interest of contemporary collectors. At a time when we find ourselves unable to resist recording the moment rather than experiencing it, a foible borne out by the amount of mobile devices held aloft at concerts, Freya's fusion of instant enthrall in the elements and then the quelled composition of creating a painting which reflects it seems somehow pertinent. Is the glancing silver light of the dying day better represented as it is witnessed en plein air, or afterwards, in the fertile circumstances of the artists' studio? Freya's art pertains to the latter, and powerfully evokes William Wordsworth's famous aphorism, from his preface to 'Lyrical Ballads', the collection of poems that helped initiate the English Romantic movement in literature: "Poetry is the spontaneous overflow of powerful feelings: it takes its origin from emotion recollected in tranquility." In this sense, Freya Horsley, a contemporary painter with a very modern eye for the sensual power of nature in a hectic world, stands foursquare in the Romantic tradition.

Greg McGee

PAGES OF ARTWORK

Poetry produces many delights. A few weeks ago I went along to an event billed as "Poetry for All", expecting something like the usual poetry open mic' night – a mixture of good poems, eccentric poems and some that aspire to poetry. Instead, it was an evening of powerful work from poets living with deafness, or autism, with blindness or experiencing prejudice against who they were, reading to an audience as diverse as the poets. Some poems related directly to the poet's experience, nearly all were accompanied by vigorous simultaneous signed translation. *Dream Catcher* is delighted to be able to feature some of the poems from that session in this issue – by Tanvir Ratul, Becca Miles, Imogen Godwin and Donna Williams – and welcomes the added diversity these poets bring to our pages.

Elsewhere, the post bag over the last few months has included, by chance, several reworkings of traditional tales: Eleanor Porter examines The Twelve Dancing Princesses; Linda Lee Welch tackles Little Red Riding Hood and Charlotte McCormac goes inside out through the Mirror on the Wall.

And there's Rage (lots of it), Fear, Love, Humour, Schooldays, Nature, Cruelty, Mystery, Vengeance, Philosophy, Illness and Death.

To finish, there's a haiku by Jane Stuart celebrating all those great troubadours whose songs shape our lives and our poetry, knowing or unknowing. Thank you Leonard, Joan, Bob, Tom…

John Gilham

1.

Too many people have feigned support
for this resistance or that
when those fights were hot,
and the damned were giving it back
only to withdraw
when the bridges broke
and people got beaten back
to their dank flophouses

It's okay to leave
Many do
but what our furious times have added
is disrespect
is indignation

There are many among us now
who, while keeping no stones unturned
to establish
that they are fighting the good fights
have added on to nasty structures,
have fed the vultures on.

Beasts that pounce from fore
are easier to fight
but they, who have
clouds & curtains of fake sympathy
to hide behind
while they advertise
smooth ways of life,
aesthetic propriety
and other endowments
that capital brings –
hold control. Hold power.
You know this.
You know them.
History is old.
There have been way too many
tiny, tingling times
when you have reached out
and their gates haven't budged
an inch

Meanwhile,
these mad wars,
of classes, races and sexes,
have raged on,
relentless.

As for the people
who have always been fucked up
by these wars,
who aren't you and me,
and who won't be reading this rant,
they know who their real enemies are –
even among those
who feign empathy
but will never build bridges
with them
except those through which they can loot more.
They know
that their darkness isn't the light
that shines on
those crockery and cutlery;
their sounds aren't the music
that fills
those houses and cars.

And as for us,
conscientious objectors,
who,
despite all criminal inheritance
have chosen not to side
with those who fan these wars
it is more confusing.
Our fake learnings
make us stick on
to false hopes
such as of finding solidarity,
even among those who masquerade too well
Beware these enlightened do-gooders
Beware their trends & traits
Beware their spaces and times
They are with those – they who claim they fight
They are with those – you who claim you fight
They are not your friends.

2.

800 thousand people
Nah! Fuck that
800 thousand phantoms
are marching towards you
right now

you have taken their lands
you have taken to hatred
you have been taken by greed
they knew nothing of this
they knew everything
their backs, painted by barbwire,
cooked by bullets
know everything.

800 thousand dreams
that couldn't connect
how the price of rice & onion
and the price of guns and tanks
and the wrath of Buddha
and the sword of Rama
Or even fucking Mo
would not let them
return to their homes by sunset,
maybe, smoke a little,
and look at the river flowing by,
clouds making shapes in reds and oranges
so they turned with the tides,
with the agony of the moon, the weeping hills,
the alert golden winged vultures – with all history and being –
800 thousand vivid humans

first you didn't count them
and now, you can't
and, right now,
in deep silence,
they are marching
towards you
towards the spot between your eyes
may 800 thousand nightmares be
all yours this evening

Rohingya, flesh of me and my mother
soul of my sweet, big, ancient earth
you,
friends,
shall live
And they, who took your lands and bodies,
shan't.

Tanvir Ratul

Let me talk to you about pride.
That glowing feeling making you all warm inside.
It's a raised glass at a wedding
And feeling your arms outspreading
A front row Dad filming a Year Three nativity
and Armstrong's first steps into zero gravity.

We know pride pretty well,
But there is a myth we must expel:
That pride must be placed onto us by others:
Our fathers, sisters and mothers
When in fact pride is something we can build ourselves
It is a movement, an ethos, that leaves no one on the shelves.
It is about Instead of letting society label and compartmentalise,
Learning we with disabilities CAN rise.
Unpack ourselves from boxes ticked:
deaf, wheelchair user, learning disabled,
mentally ill, or partially sighted
To join a species united.

Because We are all Breathers of oxygen,
feelers of feelings – and some other variables.
So let's reject sad piano instrumentals
And ask those around us to look for the people we are inside.
Not letting 'heartwarming' videos outsource our pride,
instead let's keep pride homegrown.
Not as commodity being siphoned but a seed to be sown.
Instead of being inspirational
And relieving the able's concerns for the Existential
We can be stoic, resourceful and admirable.
Not the helpless characters in a parable.
Let us not apologise for asking for the ramp.
Let this poem be an approval stamp
No one need apologise for a body built shoddily
When it is just an outcome of the genetic lottery.
Let us not need to wear badges so someone gives up a seat.
Let us not open brown envelopes with our hearts missing beats.
And instead of our partners being praised for inspirationally putting up with us,
Maybe, just maybe, we could be praised for putting up with them.
And I will say this over and over again:
Disability is not the protagonist of our stories.

Nor is it a nemesis or the source of all our glories.
Botched body, mind or something inside
We can build our own pride.
We are all human
And humans sometimes look like us.

Imogen Godwin

You wonder why
we say 'Nothing about us without us',
as you parade us about
as a backing track
to our parents' laments,
fit only to
howl and growl
and grunt and groan
as if all we are
is noise.

You wonder why
we're so afraid,
while you funnel the funds
of the scared
and the drained
to support your search
for a solution
to our existence

You wonder why
we shout so loud.
When high-functioning means
I can't speak for all of us,
and low-functioning means
my speech isn't speech,
forgive us for feeling
we aren't being listened to.

You wonder why
we flinch when you say:
'Love the child but hate their autism.'
As if we haven't heard
a version of those words
in the mouths of those
who'd torture to the tune of
'Love the sinner, hate the sin.'

And they wondered why
it took thirteen calls.
Thirteen close, close,
ear-to-the-wall,

close calls,
before they believed
my screams were the sound
of a human being
and not just noise.

Becca Miles

THESE HANDS ARE BIGGER THAN THE SKY
(inspired by Emily Dickinson's 'the brain is wider than the sky')

These hands are bigger than the sky;
the sky they contain.
The Sun and planets and moon and stars
and more, they sustain.
These hands are deeper than the sea;
the meaning they portray
goes far beyond what you can see,
as all things, they convey.

These hands are just the same as sound,
for judge them, line by sign
and they will differ, if they do,
in how they touch the mind.

Donna Williams

MY CAT

I had a cat
But she grew old and died
Time passed
I went to the cats' home
Just to have a look
The first cat was long-haired...
...but when it started to lick its arse...
The second cat was short-haired... and psychotic
The third cat was soft and sleepy
Then all at once a fourth cat...
All white...
Our eyes meet...
No. A kitten's too young, too hyper.
What's that you say?
It's deaf?
That's MY cat.

Donna Williams

I am sitting on the seawall, the black water crashing at my feet, the ocean going on forever, the big, fat gulls swooping down threatening to tear at my eyes. It gives me the heebie-jeebies.

*

Robert was at the bedroom door, a tall man with broad shoulders. He always has a growth of beard. He has a habit of hitting things with his hands, sometimes open-handed, sometimes with a fist. Walls. Doors. It seems to me he is only happy when the world is shaking. He broke the trampoline into bits in a fit of temper. I watched it all from the kitchen window. The whole thing collapsed in upon itself. He took the metal rods across his knee, bending them to his will.

I knew what he was after and when he took off his pants, I laughed, but, really, I was afraid.

He has a habit of laughing at me. Told me to get a tattoo. All bus drivers, he said, have tattoos. He thought he was better than me but I never wanted to stare at a computer all day long. He has soft hands and a hard heart.

My mother loves Robert. She invites him to dinner and dad hides behind his Sunday Times. There's a paper to hide behind. Bullets wouldn't penetrate its hide.

Robert sits at the table and chats her up. He eggs her on to drink more red wine. It's so false. He tells her she is "squiffy" which always makes her giggle and he pats her bum, following her into the kitchen while dad and I sit dumbly, wanting to die. She is an old woman with a fat bottom and a dodgy hip and he knows what I think of his behaviour but he doesn't care.

I'm told I am pregnant again but I know they've got it wrong. The facts don't add up. He took me from behind but I closed down all the openings, made my body a fortress. Mind over matter. Complete shut down.

My best friend, Ellen, is looking after me and saying nice things. She combs my hair, very carefully, in front of the fire. I know she loves me but not in that way. She repeats the story of how her brother used her when she was fifteen and how she came across this church on the island of Majorca where you place a stone in a dish and offer up a prayer for all those women who are in the same boat.

I'm thinking of leaving Edinburgh and never coming back. It would kill my dad but I have very little to stay here for. Aidan is young enough to start again. I can always get a job. They're always looking for bus drivers.

He drove me home last Sunday and he was drunk. I don't know why I got in the car, only, I suppose, with the thought of making it clear we were finished. He was after my thigh when changing gears. I wasn't wearing tights. It was very warm for autumn. All day long I had noticed the passengers huffing and puffing, the engine making the world too hot to bear.

Now he's asleep in my bed.

I call Joe, quietly, from the bathroom, my hands shaking, my mouth blubbering. I met Joe at the gym. I get an allowance to keep fit. Bus drivers have a short life expectancy. Joe lifts big weights, the kind of numbers that make your mind boggle.

He came round at three in the morning. I don't have to say anything because we had spoken in a corner of the pub where a bad draft from the door keeps people away. I told him the whole story.

"If he touches you again," he said.

Joe hit him across the head. Twice.

*

Joe lives in Newhaven. He's from fishing folk. The sea is in his bones. His grandfather died at sea. The great storm of 1998. There's a memorial down by the harbour. Joe told me all about it. Tears filled my eyes. Tiny figures cast in bronze. One mother, shading her eyes, looking out to sea, knowing the worst.

Joe dumps him in his little boat no bigger than ten pence and rows off into the darkness.

"You'll be okay," he says.

He wants me to go out in the boat with him but I wouldn't be seen dead in such a flimsy thing. Not like my big bus that can take on the whole world.

*

I walk down to the harbour most days. I don't talk to anybody except an old man with a bad leg. He knows the buses inside out and is always teasing me, saying let's run away together. He has a long grey beard and his clothes are never very clean.

I rest on the seawall. The water comes and goes, never taking a rest, giving nothing away until it is ready.

It gives me the heebie-jeebies.

Stewart J Lowe

PRIDE

Daylight catches him up
and thrusts devotion upon him
like an unwanted gift.
It lies torn open, hidden
under the bed.

It could not be refused: he accepted –
but tried to change it. Could not.
Changed his costume instead.
Bland. Waited until he felt ready
to wear his rainbow stripes.

Charlotte McCormac

CREDO

I

Imagine the tenderness –
him knowing, the others not,
or even if sensing this was the end
of the road, not rumbling
the plot. His sadness
at losing such imperfect love
such human love
love you could touch.
The crowded room, the puzzled looks,
the cooking smells.

II

Whether it happened is now irrelevant,
or how or anywhere or anytime.
Nor is it just a yearning to believe
in who we hope he was or hope he meant.
It's not really about him at all.
It's how his story makes us long to be
the sounder selves we've shaped to live the tale
which tests us daily and which leaves us wanting
its almost world, in which we do not fail.

III

We woke together to the morning light.
I heard these words like birdsong in my head.
But will they say what I have never said?
And would you understand? –
that what may be fiction must be felt as fact
to solve our loneliness, and take the hand
each holds out in that real, invented land.

Tom Vaughan

A season of gold; its rich
caress lingers on the white altar;
low sun clings to his hair;
red, not as the rose
nor as the geranium,
red as the turning leaves outside.

red also his silk chasuble and the
sanctuary lamp, flickering the heat of love.

she remembers when she crept to this altar as a child
while the sun poured autumn through each window
and she felt for the first time in her mouth
the changed elements,
a wafer mixed with wine.

his taste might startle her tongue. Like that.

Thelma Laycock

HEMINGWAY

Hemingway said that
'the mouth worried you
until you knew it,
then it worried you more'.
Well now I know the shape
and taste
of your mouth,
and with it you consume me.

You follow the curves of my thoughts
with your tongue
and taste the salt of obsession
that coats my skin.
Because 'all things truly wicked
start from innocence',
and your mouth started
with angelic nothings,
and ended with
the devil's smile.

Elisabeth Jeffreys

shadow faces rising from the pavements
everywhere are my fear
whisper of other languages
in doorways, in buildings I don't belong in
the new is what I'm afraid of
in bedrooms I shouldn't be in
children of the new age
the news is what I'm afraid of
all God's children except
I no longer believe in God and
the boundaries of human are blurring
are they brothers or sisters
if they want to kill
not me personally
they don't even see me

as it always was, political
I might deny my own but another's
is disrespectful
another, someone, you
if you come at me with a sword
and the blinding sun behind you
all you will see are my clothes
all I will see is your sword

but I can't put God in the dustbin
god(s) we have made that have shaped us
gods they have made for survival
in the heat and sand of the desert
so cruel in the name of mercy
where is the god of rain
there is a god who is always weeping
so many wrong decisions
in the muddy ditches of sorrow
no climbing out into sunlight
no surge into life with the spring
though grass is no longer a symbol
of more than matter and death

belief entwined inside
like a spinal cord articulates
all that you do and say

20

how should I disconnect you
how would I have the right
what have I got to offer
uncertainty, unbelief
I am slow-footed to follow
the dizzying whirl of change

what does a chimpanzee think
when does a foetus feel pain
how different are sex and gender
whose hand is holding the knife
the syringe, the packets of pills
are you a boy or a girl
do you have a father and mother
or either or other or both
do the questions even make sense
do I have the right to ask
another or someone or you
no longer out there somewhere else
but here implicit inside me
folded into my veins and my blood.

Kathleen McPhilemy

Fear I'll forget a meeting.
Fear I'll forget to wear clothes in a meeting.
Fear lights turning off, fear bleach not bleaching,
losing my liver, just one jigsaw piece missing.
Fear unpaid bills, and typos. *Public*
misprinted *pubic,* my name switched to Slice.
Fear pie and pi, floating extra thumbs,
fear strangulation by halo, and new hellos,
and wings without a bird. Swallowing teeth.
Fear groups and cereals, boot steps on gravel,
fear I'll remember what didn't happen last Tuesday,
fear unexplainable bruises. Fear babies
and food babies, upsizing to an empty bed.
Fear boiled sprouts, fear sprouting horns,
fear thoughtlessness and fear of thought.
Fear mispronouncing quinoa on the radio.
Fear I'll never feature on the radio.
Fear turning white. Fear fuzzy midnight
and honey stripes, fear getting stung,
falling, lifts not lifting, running out of lungs.
Fear, who struts on stilts. Fear, who wears eight legs,
Fear, who doesn't fear juggling our emotions.
Fear who never sleeps but lurks beneath
a mug of cold hot chocolate.

Alice West

THAT NIGHT...

That night, I had a spat with my soul.
The lamp, the moon, my "Marlboroughs".
Writing paper. And my desk turned ocean.
A distant sail. One of us at the helm.

What was the issue? Really, just stuff.
Above the roofs, some invisible light.
Between us down here, silence and mist.
The desk lamp dimly glowed all night.

While we observed our silent vigil
A blizzard rocked the world around us.
Streetlamps, now warships, were rocking, too.
Invisible wings moved close to my door.

'That's wings! Can't you hear them?' – 'Nonsense',
I scoffed. 'Just the draft and the darkness!'
'No, listen! It's wings!' – 'Listen up now, my soul.
Let's check – not one wingthing in sight.'

We got up and tiptoed towards the door.
Was that a draft or a whisper? Who did we discover?
'It's likely the wind, or perhaps...' – 'No, no.
That's wings there, wings! Don't you tell me...'

I pushed back the bolt. The stairwell was sombre.
Amidst the darkness there she stood: winter.

Oleg Okhapkin
translated from Russian by Josephine von Zitzewitz

White Day

There is a man. He smells of coffee. If you put your nose close to his mouth or his fingers, you smell he is a smoker.

There is a woman. She smells of honey and flowers. If you put your nose close to her neck, her hair will softly brush your face.

He is an artist, and works graphite pencils with rugged hands.

She works in an office and lifts ringed fingers to papers and phone much of the day.

They catch eyes in the rain, passing to their homes.

He enters his apartment. A pale mixture of greys, blues and browns envelop his vision. Shiny black objects wait to hum into action for him. Coffee machine is first to be used.

She is greeted by a rush of warm colours. They leap out of every room. She sits soft on the sofa, removes her socks and rubs her feet. The kettle boils.

His blue eyes focus onto a screen. He switches jeans for jogging bottoms, pours his coffee. The coffee is dark, like his stubble. His skin is heated by the steam. He unbuttons and removes his pale brown shirt, scratches his neck.

Her lips cover the mug's rim and she drinks tea. She has changed into a fuzzy light blue jumper and it makes her softness feel softer. She reaches for a box, and opens it to eat the chocolate inside. She unwraps gold foil from one, and it eats it slowly. She sips tea. She unwraps blue paper from around another and eats it quickly, devours it. Enticing violin fills the air, making the colours of the room shift and undulate.

He is tired and moves to a dark room. Blue sheets that look black in the night's shade cover his bottom half. He reaches his arm and rests it on the pillow above his head. He coughs, sniffs, sleeps.

She is tired. She moves to a room that smells of her perfume. She pulls the covers back, undresses, puts on a loose Tshirt. She goes to the bathroom, comes back to bed, and slumps in. She exhales for a long time, switches off a bed-side lamp, and sleeps.

When you watch him sleep, you see black eyelashes which match thick black eyebrows. Thin lips pop open as inside his mind, he climbs his desk to reach a window. He is pulled inside to a pool in a forest and a nymph stares at him. He tries to reach her but she swims down further than he can reach. His breath scratches his throat when he wakes up gasping.

Her sleep is calm. Behind her large eyes, she flies through greens and blues, and lands in an ocean. A whale spouts nearby and its song resonates in her chest. The whale passes close to her and she can now catch it in her hands. She opens her hands, and a frog jumps out and plops onto the sand beside her, melts into a fluorescent pink puddle of goo. She wakes, and sleeps again, until she becomes hungry.

Ness Al-Shaikhly

(Reprinted, with editing error corrected, from DC36)

There is an art to how she eludes people. It is not achieved by chance, nor through smoke or mirrors. The eyes have it – she never gives anyone a second glance. She gazes straight ahead, searches the middle distance. In this realm she loses herself and is lost to others. Except me. Her stratagems, impressive as they are, do not work on me. I see through the cloak of invisibility. I do not miss much. Her gait for instance – she doesn't so much walk as float. It is the movement of someone not pulled down by everyday gravity. Or dragged down by their illustrious past. It is the walk of the free.

It has to be her.

We will never meet of course. She does not wish to be disturbed. If ever there was a person whose body language expressed this then there she is, vanishing on the horizon.

On sunny days a wide expanse of her face is concealed by dark glasses. On wan days the bloodless skies are reflected in the pallor of her skin. Observant readers will note my observant ways. All I need is a millisecond to register everything, about a place, a face; down to tapering details. The hint of an opal at her throat, the glint of silver round her wrist. I can log an overload of details in a single moment. It's really too much.

•

'There has to be a world beyond the spotlight' – didn't she say that once? 'I just want to be a citizen'. Am I misremembering these lines?

I used to wonder what had brought her to this minor town, this pinprick on the map. Surely, with the money she'd made, she had other options, a wide horizon to explore? If the world's your oyster why pitch up at Deadsville? It made no sense to me. I would reflect about her but I don't have time for much speculation. My time is pressed: running a small cinema with big overheads, trying to stay afloat in choppy waters – this consumes my waking hours. Navigating these waters – sometimes it seems beyond me. Payment demands angling in from all sides like cuckoo beaks, my wife reading aloud bank statements like the Riot Act: alert reader – I need only sketch these details for you to see the general picture.

•

I have never made people aware of her presence in this town. Even the first few times I saw her I did not single her out to friends, or strangers. It would have felt wrong to have sabotaged her attempts to be invisible. So sterling were these efforts that it seemed that I alone could see her pass

27

by, dressed invariably in stylish attire, some gauzy black fabric, a silk scarf of the richest purple. On windy days her hair would be marshalled into a gold clasp. On still days it trailed to the mid-point of her back, a straight dark mane.

It had to be her.

Older. The childhood features that emblazoned a thousand cinema screens, embellished countless teenage walls were outgrown, and yet some trace of these remained. The high forehead, the far-away look in her eyes, the other-worldly air, exploited with such success in the *Agent Spook* films, in which she starred, spectrally, as a ghost.

In six years she appeared in nine films, the plot of each more lethal than the last. Yet she survived death-by-plot. While lesser actors were beaten down by bad dialogue, poor casting, formulaic plot twists, she prevailed. Film after film threatened to deliver a body blow to her career, and yet she weaved through it all; agile, resilient. The films were good precisely when she was on screen. It was as though through sheer force of will she could evoke a protective circle around herself, beyond which everyone else fell. The bravest, the best.

I suppose the first of the *Spooked* franchise had a fragile charm. An eleven year old girl, bullied at school, spooks her tormentors with the help of a friendly ghost. Who could forget the climactic scene when the bullies are given the fright of their lives when out trick-or-treating? Well, everyone apparently, everyone has forgotten. Except me.

Her success was loud and explosive but has left no mark. Her whole career seems had been compressed into six eventful years and then, in her late teens, the twilight years, she retired from view. Who knows what she could have achieved had she worked to a more advanced age, say twenty one? Who knows what she could have achieved given better material? But she never was given better material. She was given the script for *Agent Spook 5.*

•

The last few times I've seen her I've noticed a change. The colours of her clothing have been muted. Still stylish, but less likely to invite attention. She seems to have taken the art of elusiveness to another level, a finer point. Not just with her apparel either. She seems to be less physically...*there* now, as though, by an act of will, she's removing herself from the world. Her edges, her contours, appear less clearly defined, more nebulous somehow.

I glimpsed her leaving a gallery, dressed in subtle blues, restrained charcoals. I looked up and she was looking into my eyes, a moment's contact, a lapse on her part. In a millisecond she came to herself and looked away and yet, within that millisecond, I could see her quiet interior heaven. Then she was gone, fading up the street.

The last time I saw her she was less visible still, as inconspicuous as a window pane. She's withdrawing her presence from the world, pulling in her aura, retracting towards vanishing point. Even my eyes could barely settle on her, find her among the crowds which didn't see her. She pulled away from us all, free.

•

How can someone who was once so present have receded so much? This is the question no-one's asking. Because to ask it would be to remember, when – partly through the force of her own will – she is being forgotten.

Even now, in her late twenties, her past successes are a far-flung memory, distant twinkling lights. But she does not want to return there. I used to wonder what had brought her to this minor town but now I understand – she wants to escape, escape any lingering afterglow of the spotlight. This is her intention, her role here, one she's enacting with aplomb. It's her greatest performance; not diminished by the lack of an audience to witness it. It's a role she's perfecting. I have absolute faith in her ability.

Soon she will disappear completely.

John Vale

PIT BROW

The women wore trousers and over-frocks,
Close-fitting clothes (safe, dustproof),
That stressed each curve of breast, hip, buttock,
Rough clothes that spoke of smoothness sealed beneath.
Pent-up sexual feelings, come spring,
Would bevy forth in horseplay,
Not women hey-ho'd by men,
But a new boy hey-ho'd by the women,
His John Thomas unhoused, sized up,
Whilst he, raw fool, resisted.

Oh to have acted otherwise,
Lain back, debagged and stood,
Let them have their playful way,
And afterwards feel good!

Ben Benison

ALL THE WOMEN ARE SLEEPING

1.

My mother-in-law sleeps on the couch
while my wife is asleep in our bed
and our infant daughter slumbers
in her basket on the bedroom floor.
I walk through a house filled
suddenly with the mist that rises
from women in their sleep.

And it is as if all the women in the world
were sleeping at once,
and gathering strength to share
with our little one who does not yet
understand her hands.

Is this behavior written in the genetic code,
or scratched and painted on the inner walls of bone
where the marrow clings,
hidden in the darkness there
like the cave paintings of a private worship,
there to seep into the new-made blood
the way the paintings breathed life
into the air that rose to the cave's mouth?
It waits in a dark place
that only the blood can find
and where the blood is brought to life.

2.

My wife sleeps in our bed
and the baby sleeps draped across my arm.
Their breathing is out of sync,
but still somehow as one,
like a single wave that strikes
at different moments along a beach.
Do they dream the same dream?
Does her mother share her dream,
and teach her in it, take her hand
and say, "Look daughter, this is dreaming,
this is how you dream,
this is what dreams are made of"?

Later, the baby still asleep, I pace through the house with her
and wonder if I am working out
the wandering of her dream,
if because she cannot walk
I walk for her, my world a mirror to hers.

3.

Just the two of us, she sleeps on my forearm.
My skin feels her ribs as she breathes.
Her two arms encircle my one,
a circle joined that makes the center whole.

These are her private moments of silence,
of sleep and dreams.
There is nothing I can say
she would even hear.
So I watch, and wait for her to wake
when I will tell her
"these are your eyes opening,
this is light and darkness,
this is your father's face,
and this, all together, is the world,
and it is as wide and as open as your eyes."

Kenneth Durham Smith

You said you'd visit in the spring,
so I have prepared since January.
I coaxed the trees to bud, then leaf;
the cherries and the apples
I sang into bunching blossom;
the birds I trained to fly in circles
and as they loop around your head
to call your name.

Thinking you might come across the lake
I painted the boat with light
and rigged a yellow sail.
I fed the fish while playing my guitar
so they would rise and welcome you
when I took you on the water.

Then the flowers returned
and the sun invited me to clean the windows,
to add crisp curtains, new duvet,
to polish boards, gleam the stove, while ear-like
speakers overflowed the cabin
rehearsing for your arrival
Pastoral Symphony and Spring Sonata.

'No, no – no problem. My misunderstanding.'
With lake and birds, fish, trees and rain,
who could ask for more?
I am patient in the disciplines of love.
I'll eat the flowers.

Kieran Egan

I am tired.
So tired.

I am a jigsaw puzzle
Full of missing pieces, because
I used them to fill the spaces
You imagined within yourself.
And for every part I gave away
You hoarded your own closer to
Your chest.
And I would look,
Try and see the bits of me in you
Because I thought it would be enough,
But you painted them over.
You were fit together,
Your puzzle showed a garden;
A watercolour masterpiece
Whilst I carefully cultivated my garden
Of black – the yawning emptiness
Where I should be.
My darling I was Frankenstein and
You were my greatest creation.
I always knew you'd destroy me in the end.

Elisabeth Jeffreys

ELDORADO

It's all the rage it seems, to mine
One's language – an exploration of another time
For me – a digging down to Barnsley days,
When local words I spoke were always
Broad as each grandfather's smile.

Mining words from a past once mine,
The years of growing-up, remembered signs
Of pits – of Carlton and far Monckton's smoke,
Their mouse-grey sprawling spoil-tips yoked
Together on the sky-line.

My father mined, grandfathers too,
But not for them the hullaballoo
Of word-webs, just shifts spent at the face,
In black and dust, cramped for space,
Backs and arms like Danish Blue.

So like some lost conquistador
On a quest for undreamt wealth somewhere,
Not South America but in Yorkshire's land
I seek the golden age where I belonged,
Bright legend worth the searching for.

Andean muckstacks flying-bucket-topped
Curlered women who call in corner shops,
Red Trackies passing, the 'Pull and Push',
Disordered moments from the childhood rush
Towards a future that would never stop.

'Ey up serry, off fa sum spice?'
'I'll cadge sum coppers frum me mam alright?'
Then down to Lundwood where
A thousand chimneys throttled air,
In council clusters redly tight

To Darley's shop, and jarred in rows
Stood mint-balls, bubblies, vast treasure trove
Of jewelled sweetness sold in dunce's caps
Penny spanish in pastel seams we'd dab,
Deep kalei layers of lemon, orange, rose.

The balaclavaed days of snow at school,
Slairing, jerkins zipped and wellies full
Of slush, mauve-ringed calves, sodden socks,
When running noses meant 'Kompo for Coughs'
At home, unbidden, two bitter teaspoonfuls.

Sometimes it siled it down all day
Then indoors sluffened by the fire I'd stay,
The tin up to be safe, but culling heat
As draughts wound coldly round my feet
While at invented football games I'd laik.

Outside 'The Star' at Cud'orth men'd wait,
Rippers laiking from Grimethorpe pit,
All on't'compo', no paddy-bus for them,
Just smoking tab-ends, coughing phlegm,
Until the day became too dark to sit.

And Eldorado too, but just an ice-cream bar
From fridges at the 'Rock' or café by the park,
A polar-bear their symbol like Fox's Glacier mints,
Last dosh spent, then totally skint
In Saturday sunshine or matinee dark.

A dad on shifts of afters, days and nights,
Who early doors made clear to me the fright
Of working underground in constant black,
Whose vision of darkness now shifts me back
Caff-hearted from a long-gone life

To see rough-levelled grass where mines have closed,
Abandoned tracks of weed and dog-rose
Leading to places I can no longer reach,
From where I turned my back to seek
A fortune down far different roads.

My coins of dialect have all been spent
Too prodigally, and only an accent
Featureless remains – difficult to tell from where
It came. And so I sit like Joe Locke here
Mulling upon my discontent

To find a language mined. Rich ore has gone,
Uncovered waste remains as slagheap on my home.
There is no shining city filled with gold,
Just wagonloads of memories, hard and cold
As Eldorado ice-cream freezing on my tongue.

Ken Gambles

Those were the days of the lilac crushed-velvet cap,
tight daisy-print leggings and a white crop top,
of yellow Doc Martins, rings on every finger,
slashes of red lipstick and smudgy darkened eyes.

Love was my core, my apple seed, my creed.
I was a puppy in boots
and he, for a while, played the hero and villain.

So here we are, stepping into the stuffed carriage
sometime after lunch, the Bakerloo line and that terrifying hush
you get on tubes when everyone ignores the proximity of another being,
erecting their blank wall of protection by avoiding eye contact.
And here we are with guitar, violin and tambourine – a crowd of us –
jazzing up the air, with his voice and smile curling, snaking up legs, in
nostrils.
We shatter, we thaw, and clink – into the crushed velvet cap pours
a shower of coins, clinking, chinking. I'm holding it, pirouetting,
smiling.

Later, he counts them, in piles, like Midas. I'm not thinking of gold –
just watching his fingers, thinking of the night.

Miranda Day

Decades on you made a toast at my last supper; the one you finally
showed up to
Memories of sticky tarmac at school came flooding back
You had played cats cradle with the local girls, chewed straw under your
lip
My heart was a diamond necklace in the black glove of your hand
One raise of your palm could stop a national anthem
By this point my love for you had veins; purple and varicose
I'm relieved you never managed to lift up the veil and see my make-up
smeared, hands bone, eyes like wilted flowers
Abandoned in a loft without the luxury of light. Give it to me
Heartbreak is a storm and you had crouched in fear of lightning, but I had
let it strike me
I was disappointed that when you opened your mouth it was syllables,
consonants and adjectives that came out
We were always going to be fond memories, and no future
When we kissed cheeks I noticed that your breath smelt of white wine
And you were sprouting some fashionable hair from your ears
My conversation crackled into nothingness like candyfloss in our young
mouths
Before I opened the door to leave you caught my eye and stuck your
tongue out
You were saving face but I had the last laugh
Passion is a two-way street and I waited at the bus stop for a long time
I hadn't known you took a different route, and it was right time for me to
walk home, close the gate behind me and swallow a bitter pill.

Angelica Krikler

On Bloom Street, the light from streetlamps travelled down the roads,
escaped from view and found a home in the sewers
They had met behind the wings of a theatre; two quiet souls who knew
the dreams of stepping on stage were reserved for those who shone
And they bonded in their way. Talked in whispers, even when the
audience clapped and heckled – afraid that their connection, if found,
would be destroyed by people with big footprints, who didn't look where
they were going, dusted up by the cleaner after each show
Suzy seldom looked people in the eye, so when she did stare directly at
Frank, he knew it meant something; possibly the world
They walked back from the great big Hawk Theatre, down the sidewalks
of Bloom Street. He leant her his patchwork jacket and Suzy clutched
onto it
Trying to hold the hands of a clock, so that the moment wouldn't end and
the question would never be born
She said yes anyway.
And she called him up when she reached the fourth station, said she
didn't know when to get off
But what she really meant was, she didn't know if she wanted to
Didn't know if being Mrs Frank Parker would give her the keys to the
golden gate; if a title and a purpose was the point of life, the final
platform you're supposed to step onto
Nevertheless, Suzy walked out into November, waiting with her large
brown suitcase
It was a strange sensation when he arrived, beaming and apologizing and
inquiring if he could hold her luggage
She suddenly felt warm despite the ice in the air, like a chair had been put
behind her by the stage hand, and she could finally relax before the
curtain came up
And yet something in her sunk to the bottom of the Pacific
A month later Frank started his job at a big glass building. Suzy spent the
day painting the walls terracotta
When he came home she was lying in a bath of her own sorrow; his hand
smoothed the water's skin and retreated from its coldness
Babies came and went with lips and cheeks that felt like porridge
Suzy sang them songs from the stage, performed monologues she had
memorized and fetched their clothing, high chairs and books as if they
were props and she was the loyal understudy
Aching to have her one night on the dark mass of stage, but doing her
best to let the show run smoothly for everyone else
Until her offspring flexed and stretched into growth, tumbled from
suburbia into their own lives

The years swam in front of her eyes like watercolours and she liked to chip bits of the paint off the walls

Wedge them under her nails to feel like she was the house they lived in – was the thing that kept them warm and safe and ordinary

Suzy would occasionally go back to Bloom Street, to the theatre whose talons would always grip at her heart, until it bled out into her body, urging her muscles to react and reminding her why she had made the journey

And at the end of every show she would stand up to clap ecstatically, all the while bewitched by the lead actress' eyes, which seemed both grateful and apologetic

The same look Frank would give her when she turned round to see him still in his seat

On their walk home the rain fell like streamers from a celebration, caught red in the act by the neon shop lights. She hummed the different show-tunes

Frank stopped to buy her a pink rose, whose petals felt like the skin of her children and the colour of youth. Told her she was the greatest performer he knew

And his shaking sigh seemed to say sorry for not providing her with a life which could be advertised on Broadway signs, for not making her a leading lady

By retirement, Mrs Frank Parker had learned to find pleasure in re-painting the walls, thinking of all the coats beneath that were like pages in a book about ordinary life, about a girl who had wanted to shine but who didn't tempt fate

Letting life slowly but surely get her to the golden gates, not out of achievement, but out of acceptance

She had passed all the exams that time had challenged her with; graduated with flying colours

She allowed herself to be chucked off the train because she found out she didn't have a ticket for her chosen destination after all

Realizing that theatre may just be for those who are too afraid to act out the role life gave them; those who travelled in the direction of the bright lights on Bloom Street

Only to find they led to the sewer

Angelica Krikler

"I still can't see what I did wrong," Dennis will tell anyone who will listen.

Helen, Bright Lights' toothy allocator of companions to people unable to get to shows and concerts without assistance, will merely say, "I'll reassign you to someone else. They can be funny, some of the old ones."

He'll say, "Yes, but that doesn't mean I did anything wrong. All I was doing was helping a spider out of the bath."

"You're not supposed to help them in the home," Helen will say.

"I didn't. It's, like, a comparison. When you interviewed me I said I was the sort of person who helps spiders out of the bath."

"Oh, did you?"

He will refuse to be assigned to anyone else and will resign from Bright Lights, adding as he exits, "You may be a companion but there's no companionship."

But all that lies in the future as Helen briefs Dennis for his first – and, as it will turn out, only – stint as a Bright Lights companion. She tells him that Arnold Burnet has difficulty walking and has become nervous about driving at night. "A nice old boy who won't be too demanding for you. A widower, living by himself out at Kippen. He was managing director or something of a distiller's. Very educated." She points to the section in Arnold's application form where he writes that 'for many years the full panoply of the arts commanded my eager presence at the theatres and concert halls of Glasgow' and that he wants to 'renew the happiness those occasions have bequeathed me.'

"Pompous old fart," says Dennis, inviting a complicit giggle.

"Really?"

"Okay, shouldn't have said that. So taking him out will take me out."

"Really?"

"I read that volunteering for a charity takes you out of yourself and I definitely need that."

She drives him out to Arnold's big Victorian stone-built house for the introduction. There are framed photographs everywhere. Arnold's face makes Dennis think of a benign placid baby, but when Helen enthuses about Dennis having been carefully selected as a suitable companion, Arnold cuts her off: "He'll learn what's required."

"I'm not an office-boy, I'm a companion," Dennis wants to say, indignantly, but he doesn't say it because you shouldn't stand on your dignity when doing something for charity.

42

Arnold seems quite excited as they arrive at the Citizens' Theatre on their first outing. It's to see a play by someone called Beckett. "I wonder if Sheena Dickson is still around. I think that was her name. She used to run – what was it called, 'Friends of the Citizens'? It was part of being here, seeing her sitting at her table with leaflets and things. Glasses, quite elderly. Something so quiet and hopeful about her. It drew one in." They search in vain.

After the performance Arnold says there should have been an interval. He wants to sit in the foyer until the crowd clears. Dennis supposes that shuffling along with a stick in a crowd makes him uncomfortable. They find seats behind a protective table.

"Not sure anyone can match the standards when Giles Havergal ran the place," Arnold says. "He used to be there in the foyer greeting people like friends. There were so many people one saw all the time here. Like a club."

Movement in the crowd at the bar reveals a grey-haired woman with a gaunt face and a gash of lipstick. She's staring into her glass. The arm that holds it emerges from a slit in a loose bottle-green garment. When Arnold says, "Polly Poncho!" Dennis doesn't say he sounded like a chicken crowing.

"That was my name for her," Arnold says, lowering his voice. "Caroline thought it was disrespectful. Definitely one of the old crowd. Not looking much older, either. She was always by herself. Someone said her husband was an invalid and she was a lecturer in drama somewhere. Always in some sort of poncho thing. Always looking into her drink like someone really thinking about what she'd seen. Intellectual."

Dutiful Dennis: "Shall we go over?"

"Oh, I never spoke to her. The crowd's nearly all gone. We can leave now." He rises, his back towards the bar.

Dennis decides to say, "Perhaps she has a disrespectful name for you, too."

"Do you think so? How wonderful! That would really seal my place. What do you think it could be? Baby Face Burnet? But no, she wouldn't know my name. But perhaps someone told her my surname?"

"Baby Face Burnet the Bridgeton Brawler," Dennis says, but Arnold giggles. "Marvellous evening. Even Giles Havergal would have had a job to match that."

Arriving at the Theatre Royal, Arnold wants to tour the new foyer.

"Quite grand," Dennis offers as they circulate.

"Well, there were so many of us regulars. Subscribers. We'd see each other time and again. A family, almost. I wonder whether David and

43

Moira Lambie still come. They had an opera subscription like we did and their seats were next to ours, so we got to know them well, talking in the interval. Quite young. Went on opera holidays abroad. When they went to Verona they brought Caroline back a wee Aida doll."

Arnold appears to doze through some of the first half of something called *Rusalka*, but at the interval he's keen to get back to the foyer. Dennis gives him his arm to climb upstairs to the next level. "Just in case the Lambies are up there," Arnold says.

"Perhaps you're not recognising them because they're older."

"I suppose they would be." Arnold sounds disappointed.

Whether absent or unrecognisable, the Lambies aren't to be found, but back down on the ground floor Arnold suddenly points with his stick. "Oh yes!"

Two stylishly-dressed men well into middle age are descending the staircase, talking as if they aren't in a public place, each engrossed in what the other is saying. All of a sudden they halt and catch each other's eyes and laugh.

Arnold says, "Now *they* used to be regulars. I remember hearing one of them saying to someone that Jane Eaglen's Norma was the greatest opera performance ever seen in Glasgow. I asked him if he saw Janet Baker's Dido in *The Trojans*."

Dennis tries to steer him in their direction.

"Where are we going?"

"To say Hello to your friends."

He doesn't move despite Dennis's tug on his arm, but at that moment the bell for the second half rings. As soon as the curtain comes down at the end, Arnold is on his feet, pushing past people still in their seats. "Call of nature," he keeps saying. Dennis follows, feeling guilty because the performers aren't getting applause from him.

By the time Dennis is out in the foyer Arnold is scurrying down the stairs to the toilets. Most of the audience have left before he's back up in the foyer.

"You've been an awful long time."

"It can take a long time when you're an old man."

"I thought you'd had a heart attack or something."

"Then why didn't you come down?"

Still, Arnold seems to think the office-boy has "what's required". He lines up several further outings sooner than Dennis expects, given that Bright Lights has limited resources for buying tickets for the companion.

"But then, the old sod was rich enough to pay for my ticket," he will tell people.

At the Royal Concert Hall, Arnold stays in his seat in the interval, even though their seats are near the aisle and people who want out have to push past him. Dennis stands in the aisle, showing good manners for the pair of them. Arnold rubs his face with his hands.

"Are you unwell?"

"You get tired when you're older, Dennis." He smiles. "A man called Alan Niven was sitting five rows in front of us. Great friends, we were. One summer in the 1970s we bought season tickets to the SNO proms. Went to every single concert together. I wonder whether any of the players tonight were in the orchestra then. Lill playing the *Emperor* – at the lift-off into the last movement, one was transported into the heavens there in the Kelvin Hall, that's the word, transported, and we just looked at each other at exactly the same moment and laughed."

"We'll intercept him at the end."

"Why?"

Dennis starts to say that if he'd had a friend like that, he'd want to renew contact with him – would never have allowed himself to lose contact – but Arnold's look says that the office-boy has overstepped the mark.

"Ah, the Choral Symphony." Arnold has opened his programme.

"Is it more singing?" Dennis asks.

At the end of the concert Arnold again stays in his seat while people push past him to get out. The auditorium is nearly empty before he stands and takes Dennis's arm. Waiting at the traffic lights for the green man, Arnold chuckles. "Fancy seeing Alan Niven! It lets you know you're alive, something like that." His smile makes Dennis think of a baby being fed custard and loving it.

What will turn out to be their final outing is to a private view of paintings at the Billcliffe Gallery. "It'll be the usual suspects," Arnold says, and grins.

Dennis stops dutifully before each picture so that Arnold can study it as you should at a private view, but Arnold just shuffles past the exhibits and Dennis has to catch him up. One painting, though, does halt him. "Oh yes! Isn't that absolutely marvellous?"

Dennis finds the painting familiar – no, not the painting but the people in it – the two men he saw coming down the staircase in the Theatre Royal. In the picture, as in the opera interval, they are walking towards the viewer, absolutely absorbed in conversation. They could be two businessmen discussing a deal or two sports enthusiasts swapping anecdotes about a game, but when you let the picture enter your head you

45

see that what animates the shot of understanding between their eyes, both in the picture and back there on the theatre stairs, is love, and Dennis is an urchin pressing his nose to a window.

He looks around for the men themselves. "I don't think they're here."

"Oh, but there in the theatre, here on the walls – that's all one needs. My life is following me around!"

Dennis, deeming it part of being a companion to make conversation, says the paint is put on in a sort of broad-brush way – is that the phrase? – but you still feel you are seeing a lot of detail. Arnold, peering at the label, says, "Oh my goodness, and it's by Ewan McClure. I knew his father when I was at the university. Oh, this is delightful. What a community we are!"

Now he heads towards the tables of catalogues and drinks and nibbles, and settles himself in a wing chair placed at an angle that allows him to peep out and survey the scene. The painting of the two men seems to have whetted his appetite for some further discovery, and soon a discreet finger points towards a woman in a loose dress vertically striped in red and black.

"Miranda Aitchison!" His voice makes Dennis think of the phrase *could hardly contain his delight*. "I met her at a pottery evening class in, oh, it must have been the mid-eighties. Her marriage had broken down and she was trying to rebuild her life, taking up new interests."

She is moving conscientiously from painting to painting, glasses hanging from a cord, putting them on to read her catalogue, removing them to give each picture lengthy study: the very model of a viewer at an exhibition.

"Shall I fetch her?"

"Neither of us was any good at pottery, but we did enjoy it. Sometimes went for a drink afterwards and she would tell me about her situation." He is talking so quietly that Dennis has to stand close and lean in over the wing chair. "Her husband worked abroad a lot and then she discovered he had another woman in Brussels. Of course, there was nothing between *us*. I was married to Caroline. She just liked talking to a man about it, getting a man's angle as well as what her woman friends said. Yes, paintings were more Caroline's thing than mine. Keen on buying. Knew quite a lot of artists."

"Shall I fetch her?"

"No," Arnold says, sweetly enough, though with enough reminder that Dennis is the office-boy.

46

Dennis says, "You OK if I pop to the loo?" When Arnold nods permission, Dennis disappears into the crowd, then ducks back to the woman. "Excuse me, you're Miranda Aitchison?"

"I am." Her attention and voice swoop upon Dennis, making him feel he is a delightful addition to her evening's pleasure and can't fail to be a good person. Her hair, red glints in the rich brown, hangs to her shoulders; large red beads enhance the dramatic dress.

"I'm here with someone I think is an old friend of yours – Arnold Burnet?"

"Arnold? Here? He was the kindest man in the world to me." Her voice dances, she looks around the gallery as though nothing could give her greater pleasure than to spot Arnold.

"You met at a pottery class."

"Indeed we did. Aren't evening classes such wonderful opportunities to enrich one's life with new crafts and interests?"

So evening classes are not, after all, refuges for the forlorn, reeking of loneliness or psychological problems. Dennis thinks he might try one in the autumn.

He leads her over to the wing chair. "Look who it is," he says to Arnold, gesturing both hands towards her as she moves into full visibility round the edge of the chair.

"Hello, Arnold." From the warmth of Miranda's voice Dennis knows that the moment Arnold takes the hand she holds out, she will lean in to kiss him. Perhaps one day someone like Miranda will be as glad to see him.

"Arnold? Arnold who? Got the wrong person. Derrick McClure, that's me." Arnold rises, pushes past Miranda, pauses to glare at Dennis. "Let the past be. It's complete." He walks away, no trace of a shuffle, his stick merely carried, not used.

Dennis says, "I'm terribly sorry. I don't understand. I started this volunteering because I'm the sort of person who helps spiders out of the bath, but sometimes they run off the bit of toilet paper you're trying to help them out with. I'd better go after him, because I'm his companion."

Miranda's look radiates concern and makes him pause to explain: "Yes, 'companion' sounds funny, doesn't it? The downtrodden dependant of a tyrannical old lady. And, really, there isn't much companionship in it. But it's a charity thing, Bright Lights, we help people get to arts events who can't manage it under their own steam. No other word, really, I suppose. Not 'friend', not really, unfortunately. Not 'attendant' – makes you think of lavatory attendants. Definitely not 'escort'!" He invites a giggle.

She smiles understanding and admiration, and clearly would like to hear more from him, but, as he said, he ought to go after Arnold. By the time he's established that Arnold is no longer in the gallery, there's no sign of him outside, either. Nor is he at the car, waiting for Dennis to drive him home.

"I was only helping overcoming loss of confidence in social situations due to disabilities and his wife's death," he'll justify himself to Helen. "It was preventing him renewing contact with people who were a valuable part of his life."

"Really?" she'll say, and he'll say, "Really."

Should he call the police? But perhaps first he'd better check whether Arnold got himself home by flagging down a taxi.

Out at Kippen, your eyes are drawn across fields and farms to the evening mysteries of mountains, this being June and the sky still light, but Dennis feels like a criminal in blackest night, stars glittering and belittling, as he creeps across the lawn to a window where the curtains aren't fully closed. The view through the chink is obstructed by something on the windowsill, a small doll-like figure in vaguely Ancient Egyptian clothes, but in the background Arnold is comfortable in an armchair, perhaps even dozing. From the look of him, you'd think he'd been at home all evening.

Dennis chaps the window. That makes Arnold jump! Dennis runs and bangs on the door. Arnold opens it too soon for someone with genuine walking difficulties. At once he's the managing director. "Your services are no longer required."

"Going off like that! I nearly told the police you were missing. If you can afford a sodding taxi all out here you can afford to hire your own companion, not exploit the goodwill of people like me. Bright Lights is a charity, damn it, not your bloody private workforce. You've no fucking business making yourself a drain on Bright Lights' limited resources."

"Calm down, boy. And don't tell me that you didn't volunteer to be a companion so as to gain free access to the full panoply of the arts."

Dignity requires Dennis not to stoop to answer this, but dignity is a prison other people put you in. "The crap you dragged me to bored the arse off me. And I can't see what I did wrong." He's already walking away as Arnold says, "You tried to destroy the fellowship of the past."

Dennis calls behind him, "Pompous old fart."

Paul Brownsey

48

This morning she'd rather be anywhere else. Every Tuesday and Thursday morning it's her break duty, she knows that and has only herself to blame. She vows to keep away from the wine this evening, but then, after reviewing the day ahead, changes her mind and decides she might, after all, allow herself one, just the one. It'll be something to look forward to; a reward for teaching 10E.

She watches as Samantha and her friend Liz stroll towards her, arms linked, mouths chewing in harmony. Disapproval and sympathy contend for a verdict in her head. What is it about teenagers?

The winter sun slides behind a solid wall of cloud, cutting out the light.

"Aw right Miss? We got English wid you next, innit?"

"Yep. You'll have to stop chewing before you get through the door, though."

"Course. Ain't we doin' that book, Miss? I got mine."

"Yes. We're starting it. Well done for remembering, Sam."

"Yeah; laters Miss."

The girls disappear into a cacophony of sound. She moves gingerly towards the grass verge. Her eyes follow the streaks of glittering icy frost-spikes tracking through the playing field; a trail of silver mucus across a muddy canvas.

Her head. She would die for a coffee.

"Morning Ms. Wallace. Bit cold today?"

She clocks his heavy overcoat and the cashmere scarf, his steaming mug of tea.

Her mouth stretches. "Morning Mr Bradley. Yes, it's freezing."

"You're teaching 10E next, right? How are you coping with them?" He doesn't wait for her answer as he walks towards the staff-room. "Send Gavin over after, will you?"

Her head aches with 10E. They are a bloody nightmare and the thought of teaching them makes her stomach churn. If it wasn't for this poxy duty she could at least sit down. But, as soon as the bell goes, she'll be racing over to the other side of the building, trying to get there before all hell lets loose, determined this time, not to put up with their insults.

Fight – fight – fight!

She steps in front of Darren who might only be making a show of thumping Jasmid, but she's not sure.

Minutes later she has made the long walk to the other side of the building. Late again.

"Oy Miss, you got 'ere then? What time d'you call this? Gavin's gone for a fag!"

"10E! C'mon, get in a straight line. Josh, stop shoving!"

She's exhausted already.

"Miss, I've got to go 'n 'ave a slash." David starts to walk off.

"David, get back here! You've just had a break. You should've gone then." You bugger, she thinks.

David continues walking.

"Right 10E. Everyone in." She herds them into the classroom.

"Miss, can we 'ave a video?"

"No Josh. We going to start a new book. I told you last lesson. Who's got their 'Of Mice and Men' with them?"

Only two hands go up. Samantha and Liz are the only girls in the class. Sam's anticipated this and a thrill of triumph quivers on her fingers as she hands the boys all the spare copies.

They hate adults' voices. She gets that. If she can hide behind the voice of the narrator, they might forget her. She debates whether to show the video instead, but it wouldn't be right. She has to try, although she's unsure about how to keep their interest through the first few pages. After that, it could be okay. Human relationships. Lennie the big bear and George his reluctant protector. But, how is she going to make it through the descriptive bits? It'll be her voice telling about the sunlight twinkling over the yellow sands, the river that lies deep and green. It's all words. Hateful words.

"Fuck off, you prick! Miss he's got my book!"

"Liz, don't swear. Ryan give her her book back. Now!"

Ryan throws the book at Liz. "Mine's fucked. I wan' a new one."

"Miss! He can 'ave mine. Me an' Liz'll share."

Sam walks over to where Ryan sits. There's a serene expression in her beautiful dark eyes which quietens him as she offers him her book. It has a shiny new cover and there's no swear words scrawled over the first page.

"Well that's very kind of you Sam. I wish we all had the same attitude!" She looks at her watch as Sam returns to her seat. Panic. Is she the only teacher anywhere who takes the whole lesson getting everyone sat down?

"Right, let's look at the cover first. What does it tell you? Darren?"

"Two blokes, Miss. One of 'em's stuck right behind the other one. They're gay in't they Miss?" He leans over towards Josh and they snigger.

"Okay, okay. No, in the story you'll find out they're not gay. Anything else?"

Sam's been reading the blurb on the back. "Miss, I reckon they're migrant American labourers. One's called George an' the ova one's Lennie. He's the stupid one."

"You're gay!" shouts Ryan. "I seen you and Lizzie at it...."

Sam is over the other side of the classroom before she has time to react. Her long fingernails scratch at his face and she pulls his hair.

"Ow! Geddoff, you cunt!"

"THAT'S IT. OUT!" she points at Ryan and then to the door. "GET OUT, NOW!" Ryan, violent, punches the desk and his chair hits the floor as he stomps out, swearing. She closes the door behind him.

The class is quiet. For the first time there is no noise. Her heart is beating fast, so fast. Her eyes ache and she feels like shit.

She breathes. "Okay we'll start now. Everyone has to listen carefully because I'll be asking questions. Okay?"

"A few miles south of Soledad, the Salinas River drops in close to the hill-side bank and runs deep and green."

She looks up, and continues, her body is tense, preparing for the first casual interruption. At first, she is guarded and watchful, as she tries with all her sincerity and conviction to evoke the beautiful, idealised scenery of the setting. But soon, her voice starts to express the beauty and the truth of the words as she gains confidence. The long sentences flow, languid and slow, rising up like a blessing, before settling on them all, invoking a feeling of grace.

The bell splits through her voice and in the first few reluctant seconds all of them fade away from that world and enter more prosaic territory.

"I want all the books back, here on my desk please." Her loudness breaks their quiet.

Chairs scrape and they rush forward, pushing, pulling. Gavin retrieves a football from his back-pack.

"Gavin, Mr Bradley would like to see you in his office, now."

He gives her an offended look.

"What've I done?"

"I've no idea. He didn't tell me."

He shrugs, collects his football off the floor and runs out onto the field where a group of boys charge at him. They've been waiting for the ball. She watches and decides not to bother. Her stomach thinks her throat's cut. She heads off in the direction of the canteen.

Gay McKenna

Remedy

Feather edged and fragile,
unfurled by brisk twists of the handle,
the shavings spiral into a mound
accompanied by the crumbling graphite,
silvery specks scattered like thunder flies
within the murk of the pane.

An unlikely object of glamour –
screwed to the desk, its paint chipped from use –
I dream of being allowed to use the sharpener.

She hands me my pencil in a plump, freckled hand,
offering me her efficiency;
I inhale the scent of wood, admire the precision of the point.
Standing before her on the faded blue of the carpet,
my scuffed shoes matched to her swollen feet,
I can only think how marvellous it must be, to be a teacher.

Ali Pardoe

Unshuttably stuffed, the mouth of the Head
of Latin's briefcase gapes with irrelevance:
indifferent Caesars, redundant gods,
a language nobody speaks.
Marking crocks his other arm.
The bell delivers him on cue to 5L1.
Heeling and elbowing in, he bellows Virgil,
eclogue number five, and is ignored,
incensed at our obsession with the snow.
What's another blizzard in a winter such as this?
Whole class detention, Friday after school.

He swivels on the balls of his feet,
scribbles the fifteenth of March.
The very furniture looks bored.
Forty desk-lids open wide – an epic yawn.
There's nothing like synchronised slamming
to smother a shot, the singular spat
of an airgun's report.
Gaius Caligula Caesar drops his chalk.
Clawing the wall, clawing the small of his back,
silent as the snow's unhurried drift,
the blackboard slows him to his knees.

Phil Connolly

He sat, ashen, his thunder-furrowed brow
glowering in the shadows, on the right
of a stage that seemed to rise like a prow
over the black waves of baby-armed boys.

Not the chief, not the battle-axe loudmouth;
but the best, the one you wouldn't fuck with.
The one who would gloom dispassionately
down into the breakwaters' snaking hiss,
shieldless – not even running – trudging,
nearly, to the blood-work, the killing trade.

We dreaded getting him. *Oh shit, please not him.*
But we did. English. And he was brilliant:
hag-breath on the heath, Huck's terror-flood in the hut;
but best of all, Hrothgar and Heorot,
the battle-sweat and the claw, limbs ripped off
like timbers, the fog-sunk mere, cached landscapes
smashed open, the ravenous oceans wealthing out.

Like a night-raid, to be back after Christmas.
The sea flat as a drum, no shielding storm;
just some fore-words shingling, then the attack.
I pictured a single massive axe-hack,
not like a bowhead thrashing in its ropes,
not like the gross flow of the Ouse sludging up,
clotted with carnage the pulse couldn't clear.

Unimaginable that he could be killed.
And unthinkable, the hurt I breathed in
then; unspeakable as carving a man
open, as if with a stroke of a pen
– the spine cracking, the cage splitting like pages –
so his spirit flutters out only now.

Iain Twiddy

1959

I knew they were talking about me when their treble voices drifted in through the tiny gap at the top of my window. I was alone, putting away my books and thinking about the long walk on High Street in the footsteps of the Romans which Esther and I planned to complete that weekend. Little Susie Marks, the brightest of the children, had stayed behind and told me earnestly, 'I can understand the *words*, Miss Errol, because some of them are not very different from English, but I can't understand how they all fit together'. Perhaps one day she will, perhaps she'll make a scholar, but there isn't much in Caesar's commentaries on the Gallic wars to appeal to twelve-year-old girls. Dido and Aeneas, they'd much prefer that. I told her to look carefully at the endings, dismissed her and then I overheard one of the little wretches on her way home say, 'I'm not going to be a teacher when I grow up, because none of them ever get married.' And another, 'I expect they would have liked to. Miss Carpenter was engaged to Miss Errol's brother, but he was killed in the First World War, and they've lived together ever afterwards.'

Whoever told them that?

1911

But in those days I wasn't the Latin mistress, *magistra Latina*, but a person they could never visualise, little Lizzie Errol running about the farmyard, reluctantly rounding up the cows. Father was filling in the census, it was my twelfth birthday and the day before my sister Barbara's wedding, and I was wondering how much longer I would be allowed to stay at school. That was the second of my sisters to get married, so Maud (three years my senior) was to take her place in the dairy. And after Maud got married, it would be my turn.

My mother had had nine children, but three of them died, including two boys before I was born, so I was probably not the most welcome arrival. The fourth girl. I did have two more brothers, George, eighteen months older, and Joe, nearly two years younger. We lived then on a farm near Ullswater, to me the most beautiful place on earth. I walked two miles to the village school and back and loved to hear stories about the Romans. They'd got as far as the Lake District, Miss Fosse said, and it struck me even then that the shape of the fells and the moon's reflection in our tarn would have looked the same to them as to me. But when I was ten we moved to a dairy farm in Bedfordshire. Flat, boring, cabbage fields as far as the eye could see; I hated it. My mother, too, hadn't wanted to move so far from her family; it was done for financial reasons.

I stayed at school, invariably top of the class, while Maud went on working, happily enough, in the dairy. When the war started, George was nearly seventeen, Joe coming up to fourteen. We did quite well out of it, although Father was very angry with George when he said he hoped it would last long enough for him to go. My mother was almost hysterical.

'They're *not* going! I'm *not* losing any more children!' (My little sister Ann had died in 1913.)

'It won't happen,' Father said. 'I can get George excused; they always let the farmers keep one son.'

'And what about Joe?'

'We'll just have to hope it stops before he's of age.'

It didn't stop, it went on for four more years, and half the families we knew, both where we lived now and among our friends in the Lake District, were losing sons. I was sent to board in Bedford and get on with my studies. I saw the Highlanders march through. I kept my head down, continued learning all I could, and Miss Scrivener asked my parents to let me train as a teacher.

'She'll need to earn her own living, Jack,' Mother said, 'there aren't enough young men now for her to marry.' (I was the plain one of the family, big, raw-boned, rough-voiced; I still am.)

They agreed; they didn't want to be told that I could leave school and work on the land instead of Joe, but in fact the Armistice was announced just before he turned eighteen. Father died in the 'flu epidemic that same winter, and George took over the running of the farm. I stayed at home for another two years to nurse Mother, who was very frail by now, and by lamplight, I polished my Latin. After she died Maud, against all expectation, got married, to a man who had come back with one arm and one eye, and George said, 'It's your turn now, Lizzie.'

I told him I was getting out. He didn't believe me at first and said, 'Then who's going to do the dairy work?'

I said, 'You can marry Ivy. You've kept her hanging round long enough.'

He did, after a bit of grumbling, but I went away and got my qualifications. I moved to the grammar school where Esther was already teaching English, not actually in the Lake District but as close as I could get. I see my brothers and sisters from time to time, but my real life is here. Esther and I share a cottage, seven miles from town, and go fell-walking every weekend. They are all clever girls, the A stream. I suspect that they don't really like my lessons, the dry declensions and the gerund and the past imperfect, but the ancient Romans set me free.

2017

'It's odd,' said Susie Marks, who had been Susie Robertson for the last four decades, to her oldest friend Daphne, 'but you remember that story about how Carpenter was engaged to Errol's brother, who was killed in the first war?'

'Oh, yes. We all thought it was very romantic.'

'Well, I looked her up on the 1911 census when I was researching my own family. She was quite an interesting old thing when you got past that gruff exterior. I'd probably never have become a linguist, but for her.'

'She's dead, of course. Well, she'd be over a hundred.'

'Yes. She only survived Carpenter by one year.'

'Do you think they were – ?'

'Not necessarily. There were so few men left by that time that the women had to prop each other up. But whoever circulated that story, it's not true. I did quite a lot of research, and I'm certain. She had only two brothers, George and Joseph, and they both lived well into the twentieth century.'

'So why did the story get around?'

'I don't think anyone really knows about the dead.'

Merryn Williams

THE ELEVENTH HOUR

At the eleventh hour the band spills from the van
tugging red tunics to a snugger fit,
shouldering drums and giving fifes a shake
and then they're off.
And after them the mayor and corporation – men tied,
suited, but not to this; ladies, skirted tight and shod
in crippling heels, focus on not falling.
None of these has seen war nor marched
beyond the road's end.

Hand tapping unsteadily to the thump of the drum,
he's wheeled along at the rear,
the only one here who's been at the front.
Massed fifes shriek like shells
and the rattle of percussion bells is the sound of smashed glass falling.
Wind makes the last leaves tremble.
It's time that's defeated him, folded him
into that chair.

He bears the weight of his medals and wonders, perhaps,
who the hell we are.
We women are strangers there. We walk the long way round
and stand towards the back
for the laying on of wreaths. The blunt memorial gives heaven the finger.
This is the last post. And we weep: for the lost youth of our fathers, lost;
for sons who do not need us now; for how
soon the road's end looms.

Susan Wallace

Dead birds sing on the battlefield, though there's little to see. There's an information board and a guided walk, a shed with finds under glass: musket balls, dull beads, rusted buckles, a ring that looks too small. From the air, walls emerge from forgetfulness, earthworks bloom in subtle rings, deeper than the plough or detectorists' trowels, but all you see is a dustsheet on an old table, a worn game board with every piece lost. Around 5.30, an amateur historian turns off the fluorescent strip, locks away the war for another night. When there's nobody to hear them, do dead birds still sing?

Oz Hardwick

Good Friday to Easter Monday
The Aldermaston Research Establishment
45 miles
to Trafalgar Square
head of the column
Bertrand Russell   JB Priestley
AJP Taylor   Canon John Collins
BAN THE BOMB
united by a cause and in holiday mood
students   pensioners
pram-pushing housewives
Marxists   Trotskyists
Militant Tendency   Pinko lefties
a surfeit of duffel coats
Methodists   monks   Roman Catholics
Quakers with stout boots and stunning daughters
pacifists and vegetarians
BAN THE BOMB
stewards with loud hailers and litter bags
puzzled but genial policemen
banners   placards   pamphlets   slogans
FREEZE THE ARMS RACE   NUCLEAR FREE ZONE
PEACE FOR THE PLANET   MAKE LOVE NOT WAR
NUCLEAR WASTE FADES YOUR GENES
DISARM   DATLEG
unions' intricate embroidered regalia
a rash of CND badges
BAN THE BOMB
overnight stops in schools   church halls
swollen ankles   sweaty feet
rows of sleeping bags   hard floors
queues for lavatories   queues for food
BAN THE BOMB
last day thousands upon thousands
a fat snake bunched up and shuffling
through halted hooting London traffic
a thin snake
stretched
jogging
to catch up
trad jazz bands   drums   guitars   brass
chanting   communal singing

The H Bomb's Thunder   The Family of Man
The Saints   Down by the Riverside
BAN THE BOMB
Albert Memorial lunch break
entertained by many nations
in national dress
singing national songs
dancing national dances
slow   slow   progress
past cheering crowds   hostile groups   the merely curious
Nelson   lions   pigeons   fountains
speeches   roared applause   speeches
Michael Foot   Fenner Brockway
The Bishop of Southwark
Nagasaki   Strontium 90   Hiroshima
BAN THE BOMB

Alice Harrison

THREE HEROES OF THE GREAT PATRIOTIC WAR
"Everyday, look up."- Old Maoist Maxim

Three old women sit on a wooden bench
Their hands; quiet now, clasped together on the straightened woollen
fields of their skirts
Their grey hair covered almost perfectly by headscarves
in the manner of old women since time began

You think –
The stillness is in them as much as it is in the nature of the still image
The gift of time is weight
Layers of slow moving matter earned through survival and
the joyous, fleshy wattles of neck and arm
portray:
The decent outcome of gravity born with good posture
and warm smiles
as though they are amused by something,
or everything

But these earth heavy old women flew

Behind them on the wall is another portrait
The same three in neat uniforms among the out-dated planes
Young but just as still in time of crisis
When they were three of many heroes of The Great Patriotic War;
When they fought tyranny, for tyranny, and for hope, family, pride and
the blinding future

No deadening of feeling can be seen in the eyes now
Under the thickening hoar frost of cataract

Small quiet monuments almost forgotten.
The truth of their presence too simple to view for long.
They have something to tell
from their place at the centre of history
where all politics and war is captured in the force of their gravity,
You think

But the portrait is completed
And they are gone to make tea
The image is fixed but your eyesight begins to fail

Later it will rain and they will be glad of their headscarves
On the short walk back to the world

Jamie Lynch

LIBERTY

Why
        doesn't the
                Statue
                        of Liberty
dance?
        She never
                even looks
                        round.
People stare
        out from her
                cool
                        head.
Isn't
        her arm tired?
                Isn't her
                        torch cold?
Rock in
        the harbour:
                call that
                        Liberty?
How long
        has she
                been this
                        way?

Charles Douglas

Mirror ball snow scatters up walls and the bar blushes at its own clichés. It's 80s night with a syn-drum beat, stiff with hairspray and sharp creases; two-for-one cocktails with palm trees, ice and curly straws. Cold knees shuffle below ra-ra skirts, and flicked fringes blinker Lady Di eyes. It's a fancy dress fantasy, a Smash Hits spread; glossy as strawberry lippy, sticky as Castaway kisses; Blitz pants billowing to the insistent beat of truncheons on riot shields, rocks on paving slabs, fists on coach windows, and the familiar chorus: Scab Scab Scab.

Oz Hardwick

When men took nothing to the hill
but necessary gear,
reaching corries where plucked rock
shreds noise and folds it into cracks

(so once they rested all they'd hear was blood
flowing through their ears)
did they complain incessantly about the quiet?

Now that age tries to defend me from the hills,
I want to know which sounds excited you
when you left the corrie's mouth –

the bass and kettle drum of melt over rock and stone?
A jay's broken bassoon? Ptarmigans' punctured horn?
A breeze orchestrated through closed and open trees
until its blood-red lingering drew you deep?

Or perhaps only the pebble-pianos'
abrupt abdication of their future,
dissipating in a devil's trill of washed-out green?

But you choose to listen to a plastic sing-along.
In silence or nature, what are you so afraid to hear?

Grahaeme Barrasford Young

A creeping terror underlies the calm.
You brew the coffee, get the paper in
but something in the air provokes alarm.
The headlines scream, another day begins.

You brew the coffee, get the paper in.
December and the lavatera blooms,
the headlines scream, another day begins.
In Shishmaref the ice melts way too soon.

December and the lavatera blooms,
the sun is shining on the dewy moors.
In Shishmaref the ice melts way too soon
and thermokarsts are opening like doors.

The sun is shining on the dewy moors.
You climb up, finding diamonds everywhere.
The thermokarsts are opening like doors –
this afternoon, you're tempted not to care.

You climb up, finding diamonds everywhere
but something in the air provokes alarm:
another lukewarm winter underway.
A creeping terror underlies the calm.

Linda Lee Welch

Home time, Broad Green, Liverpool, 1950 – out of a rainswept schoolyard,
through a jangling door and into a sticky heaven. And there beneath a naked bulb,
behind a row of thick glass jars, stood Mr Cakebread with his scoop,
tipping the Salter Scales over the quarter-pound of aniseed balls for a penny.

Gobstoppers, blackjacks, Trebor Mints, dip dab, Yorkshire Mix,
chocolate-pink-and-orange-sandwich-biggies, bubble gum and acid drops.
The mysterious jujube, too hard to chew. Packs of pink and pastel-blue refreshers,
sharp as an angry smack across your face.

What never crossed my mind was who had tilled the Caribbean fields
and cut the sugar canes. And who had worked the rolling mills that pressed
the cane to pulp and mashed the cane juice bubbling in the vats.
I never thought to ask. All I asked was what a threepenny bit would buy.

In 1950 wages were reduced by a penny in the shilling. Windows were smashed
and motor cars damaged. The Governor was jostled and struck. The Riot Act was read
and the crowd fired upon, killing two men. At midnight a British warship arrived
and a state of emergency was declared ...

The women gaze out across the bay, wearing liquorice allsorts headscarves,
talking of washing machines and laughing at bad luck. They have the scent of molasses
on their clothes. A ghostly hand traces a signature on a bill of lading. Long-dead
workers in the boiling houses lour, their anger burning slowly down to ash.

Nick Boreham

MODERN GOTHIC

In pallid imitation
of the dappling of sunlight,
there's a random patterning of paler
patches where the bleach has dripped upon the mat.

The grouting,
even where the black mould
hasn't reached, is grey and peeling;
there, beneath the grimy tide mark of the bath,
flare dark stars where the white enamel has been shattered.

Something
in the warping of the mirror
lends a wry despair to every face,
and leads the eye to where the cabinet spills
hair-encrusted razors and the half-used boxes of prescription pills.

So that's the bathroom;
now you've seen the whole one-bedroom flat.
The rent's £2,000 a month, excluding bills, paid in advance.

Oh, think about it, yes –
you'll need to hurry, though;
a place like this'll be snapped up in no time,
mark my words.

Peter J King

I AM DUSK

Silently I usher in infinitesimal
changes of light, a distinct
tickle in the nostrils.
I nestle the mallard's beak
beneath the wing, bring the otter
to flex its liquid muscle
in river and pool.

Sometimes I quiet thoughts
sometimes winkle them out
like black slugs.
I am heartsease
and heart breaker
a comforter of open arms
a settling shroud of alone.

I borrow small cupfuls of time from
both ends; if you would sojourn
within my transitory boundaries
you must pay attention
be the complete observer
or I may sift between your
fingers like mist, be gone.

Patricia Leighton

71

THE FIELD

February.
Poplars recede into purple fog.

A man in hi-vis tests
the margins of his industry.

He can see no further than
his outstretched hand and

does not know how
to live beyond it.

Close by or, maybe, way off
in the distance

someone else's dog barks
into nothing – then gives up.

The ghosts will not
be corralled.

C M Buckland

1

Leave the city
        By kissing gates;
Here where the ring-road
Devours its tail,
Tar at the end of its tether,
        Hawthorn and heather
Will pick up the trail.

Follow a red thread
        That runs here:
Fuses the rowan and rosehip,
Flares in fireweed and ferns;
        Then, as
Purple swards unfurl,
Follow the ribbon of limestone,
Leading light
        On this royal floor.

2

While daylight
Frays on the brambles,
Flags our rovings and rambles,
Take the wind's unbridled way –
On paths less trampled
        By paraphrase.

From the stream,
        A lucent bed,
Rise to find the fountainhead
Forcing the rock face above:
See it leap
        From crag to cove,
Sheering the side of the fell;
Go to fill your cup with this –
The plenitude,
        The always pour.

73

3

Climb the ladders
      Of slate,
Layers that greyscale the landscape;
Scramble the scree slope
      To stagger the view:
Patchwork of drystone and pasture,
Kestrels that cross-stitch
      The torn strips of blue;
Watch for the cloudbank to sunder:

Come-down of light
      On the uplands,
Gleaming on glitters and gills;
Breathless here
      On this narrow sill,
Stand back to bird-eye
            The wonder.

Daniel Gustafsson

ENTER THE HALLS OF THE KINGDOM
- *after George Mackay Brown*

The first is the skeleton of a whale
carried up beyond the reach of tide
A floor of dry sand and kelp
that whispers like paper
the walls desiccated skin stretched
between the arching ribs
This is a hall for crawling through
til birthed like Jonah on a foreign shore

The second is the wreck of a ship
hull up to the sky, long from the sea
The planking drilled through
by beams of light, and eaten
by lichen, fungus and moss,
the slowest moving waves,
the darkness a home for toads
This is a hall for laments,
for the fish that died in the holds,
the men swept from the decks,
and the long days drowned in the wake

The third is the ruin of the Laird's house,
the walls massive stones that surround
the wreck left as the roof
took out all the floors below
A well of light and glittering rain
received from an endless open sky
This is a hall for dancing,
home to linnet, lark, and nightjar
dry cough of fox, croak of owl

Kenneth Durham Smith

Imprinted

Beyond the hedge around the car park,
on the Abbey Lawn, a front row bench,
mid-morning and the sun already high.
The peace releases birdsong in the trees,
a breeze rustling their summer dresses.
The cedar and the beech take their cue,
grasp hold of the sky's blue for balance,
reach down, sweep the grass and bow,
a gesture of homage to the square tower
looking out from a thousand years ago,
intent on a further thousand – mid-voyage –
set against the contrails of earthly journeys,
its gaze fixed on the heavenly continent.

Cedric Pickin

We're heading into the fens. The ditches'
wet net, the bared catch gasping in the wind.
Heading out, under hard-anchored cloud,
where the October leaves shoal and shiver,

where the hedgerows bristle, and a skylark
trickles by the dwindling ford; heading out,
to stand at the edge of what is not yet
a beet field's rows of regimented heads,

not yet the stench of pesticide sweeping
in like a tide. We're heading again further out,
deeper in, to where earth is all airfield,
the east wind all blaring take-off above

that draining, delving sense there must be more
than the slowly dissolving horizon,
something more nourishing to discover,
surely, where depth is everywhere surface.

Iain Twiddy

Car bumpers pranging, cyclists slanging,
hot dough, espressos high-five the air.
Kindles and headphones, flash drives and iPhones
sprint to the station, just seconds to spare.

Push-chairs trundling, toddlers tumbling,
bundles of 'narnas, nappies and wipes,
three for a pound yer oranges brightly,
sunlight painting the gates in stripes.

Buckets of lilies, hostas and chillies,
oysters, crustaceans ice wet on the slab.
Second hand gown 'Too small to fit dummy',
boxes of gimcracks well worth a grab.

Ladies who lunch, breakfast or brunch,
stories to swap and diaries to clear.
Slow cappuccinos, biscotti, new chinos
and how many Ks in his bonus this year.

Samples to try, antiques to buy,
armoires and hip baths with lions-paw feet.
Bookshops and framers, vets and Spec Savers
cat's cradle down, right and left, street by street.

Men up ladders, pounding their hammers,
refurbished, refitted, there's money to make.
Crick crack goes the patter, the fact of the matter,
prices are racing and no mistake.

Fit young tryers, City high flyers,
faux Doric columns for first-time dates.
Cocktails and spritzers, pretzels and mixers,
mobiles vibrating, then *WhatsApp* your mates.

Black cabs rumble, stilettos stumble,
George at *Bar One* stacks up the last chairs.
Sirens are bawling, drunk boys cat-calling,
retching on corners as if nobody cares.

Deep melt of night, no-one in sight,
wisteria silently creeps up brick walls.
Lost cat prowling, lone dog howling,
as the milk-float makes its first morning calls.

Claire Booker

They walk with ships
Of narrow laths and nails,
Unstably engineered
With simple love.
It is an autumn afternoon,
Late Sunday,
And sky of chill Atlantic grey
Already darkening.
Across the colliery rails
They move unspeaking
Towards the slag-heap loom
whose foothill ponds
Are deep and menacing.
They long to see their craft float
But know once gifted to water
Will be irretrievable.
Nudged into a funeral murk
Their childish vessels teeter
Then are gently borne on liquid coal
Drifting into blackness,
Like Arthur's barge
On the journey to Avilion.

Ken Gambles

As she stares into her magic mirror,
purple smoke and the king's voice rise:
she is not the fairest of them all,
and so the beauty contest begins
with a *tale as old as time,*
in which she sleeps for one hundred years.
She finds herself in a glass coffin:
her matching glass slippers fell off,
although they're supposed to fit perfectly.
The clocks strike midnight.
The façade melts to pumpkin rags when
she returns to her evil step-mother.
She *whistles while she works;*
hoping that *someday her prince will come.*
She'll prick her finger or bite the apple,
so don't bet on the prince.
He's probably a frog anyway.
She supposes she'll have to kiss him
to fly on his magic carpet.
She will fall in love at first sight,
like she did *once upon a dream;*
because she keeps on believing,
the dream that she wishes will come true.

The dream that she wishes will come true
because she keeps on believing.
Like she did *once upon a dream,*
she will fall in love at first sight.
To fly on his magic carpet,
she supposes she'll have to kiss him.
He's probably a frog anyway,
so don't bet on the prince.
She'll prick her finger or bite the apple,
hoping that *someday her prince will come.*
She *whistles while she works.*
She returns to her evil step-mother.
The façade melts to pumpkin rags when
the clocks strike midnight.
Allthough they're supposed to fit perfectly
her matching glass slippers fell off.
She finds herself in a glass coffin
in which she sleeps for one hundred years,

with a *tale as old as time*
and so the beauty contest begins:
she is not the fairest of them all.
Purple smoke and the king's voice rise,
as she stares into her magic mirror.

Charlotte McCormac

FROG PRINT

"I liked
          being
                    a frog,"
                              the prince admits.

"Sitting
          on the broad
                    leaf, I was
                              within

touch of things,
          needing
                    fewer
                              decorations

or decisions –
          beside
                    the still
                              pond, so

simply letting
          be, as
                    a matter of
                              form,

no cranky
          advisors. I'd
                    be there
                              now, if

I had not
          so much
                    longed
                              for kissing."

Charles Douglas

85

I said to Mama, I won't be long
there's a rave at Granny's tonight
and I've got to get there early.
Mama said, Keep your hood up
and watch for wolves.

I set out excited through the woods
through jasmine, creeper, belladonna.
Can't resist a flower, never could
so I started on a posy, Granny'd love it.
I heard she was a hippie once.

What I didn't know: a big bad wolf
had caught my scent. Besotted,
he took Granny by surprise and lay in wait,
cross-wired her sound system, stole her music,
sharpened his teeth on her bones.

I got there too late. The crowd were high
on E's and wine, didn't notice Wolfgang
at the controls making wild canine music
all his own. He saw me and pounced.
I hardly knew what hit me, lost my coat,

my sandwiches, my soul. That
was the first time. Ever since, I've felt
some sweet nostalgia for the wolf.
After all, he must have loved me loads
to go to all that trouble.

Linda Lee Welch

> *Then the King made it known to all the land, that if any person
> could discover the secret, and find out where it was that the
> Princesses danced in the night, he should have the one he liked
> best for his wife, and should be king after his death; but if
> anyone tried and did not succeed, after three days and nights, he
> should be put to death.*

Andrew Lang, 'The Twelve Dancing Princesses', *Red Fairy
Book*

The King

If I hadn't happened to pass by, they'd have simply kicked him back
down the stairs. A brute like that, they smirked, with clay under his
fingernails, asking to see the King! But, I thought, let him try, who's to
care when his head hits the basket? Far less bother afterwards with one
like that. I had so little hope left. And it amused me to watch the court's
revulsion. I was growing weary. All that ceremony and mess. Another
dead boy.

I should have thrown it all in long ago, consoled myself that while the
sun shone they obeyed me. There was no outright defiance. No man, not
a prince, nor a servant saw them err. But I did so want them back.

They'd never lacked for anything. Not a thing. The finest dresses, jewels,
a dainty palfrey in the stables. Best dancing masters in the world. And
they'd turned out well, true princesses, every one. Such pretty ways.

Their mother was the same. All seeming perfection. Voice of a
songthrush, light as a feather on my arm. But, there, right there, in the
thick of men's esteem, I'd watch the laughing flit of her gaze from smile
to smile and all of a sudden sense that all the pomp and obsequies of the
court, my royal crown, our vows, were insubstantial to her. Froth and
flummery. We were players in a masque. It was only when she sang, it
was only when I overheard the high clear notes of the songs she sang
alone… Well, that was long ago. She has been dead for years. Still, I
keep the window in my chamber a little ajar, so that when I wake I can
hear the birds and dream.

It took me a while to realise something was up. Blamed the tailor who
sewed their silken slippers, bid him find better leather, called him a
cozener, said I'd have him whipped. Each morning I locked the tattered
things up in my great oak chest, kept the key on my belt, but the soles
whispered to me all the same, of dancing, dancing.

I asked my daughters where they went, of course. 'Oh papa, sweet papa, all we can do is play and dream. You know the doors are bolted, you bolted them yourself.' I raged. I posted guards. I threatened. It was no good. Their minds were threaded with enchantment; I didn't need counsellors to tell me that.

At least they were intact. I had that checked.

Their dreams should have been my own. I had raised them to grace the arms of princes and be the admiration of the world. Where did they go at night that I could not follow?

The Youngest Princess

The dance has many steps and we know them all, my prince and I, we keep perfect time, round and around. What grace, he murmurs, holding me lightly, securely. I smile at the lights and the music and the beautiful people and we follow the steps of the dance.

I don't blame my father, he has to try and stop us. Every morning I see him sigh over our slippers as he places them in that big trunk of his. He stopped asking months ago; his gaze slides across us at breakfast to the long window and the slender tree that grows up towards his chamber. Then he sees me watching and he smiles. My prettiest, he says, patting my hand.

All our watchers are ridiculous. Outwit some twittering girls they think, why it's barely a task at all. They drink their wine and off to sleep they go. Sometimes we poke them a little. One we undressed – it was my idea! We couldn't help laughing: it was a little bit disgusting, such a smelly, flippy floppy thing.

And so tonight my father the King appears as usual with his champion. But what a joke! A great dark bulk of a man glowering at us in dirty boots. And he's old, there are lines all around his eyes. He'll be easy, he looks like he hasn't slept in weeks.

It should be a young man. Young men yearn to break enchantments; it is their dream. They should be prepared to die in the quest. All the stories say so. I asked my eldest sister if we too should be happy to die for our dream and she said another kind of death awaited us. She's no fun anymore. I think I would die for it. In the world beyond the door the trees are silver and gold and the light they throw makes the brilliants in my hair sparkle. My gown sweeps the fallen leaves as I walk, but there will be no spiders, no sticky mud. We tell one another there might be ghosts in the shadows and the thought makes us giggle, but it is like gasping at a play. All is delightful, no blood will flow.

Tonight's watcher went to sleep like the others but my eldest sister made us leave him be. He has a scar above his eye and his sword is notched and scratched, not light and gleaming like our princes' swords.

We walk down through gold and silver forest towards the lake, where the princes wait to row us to the dance. They are always waiting. How my prince adores me, desires me, me, above all the others! Soon he will sweep me over the water and I will stare into his dark, dark, eyes, beneath the crescent moon. Or perhaps grey. Yes, I think they will be grey, tonight.

But when I delicately step down into the boat, it rolls. A flicker of surprise crosses my prince's face. He bends and pulls at the oars so slowly all the others arrive at the castle before us. 'What ails you, my prince?' I ask, and he frowns a little. There's a bead of sweat on his lip. This is not right.

Later, in the waltz, there's a different note in the perfumed air. Wet grass, clay. Do my sisters notice? I try to put it out of my mind. I keep on dancing, I smile at my prince and he smiles back at me. Everything glitters.

Only, this morning, when I wake, there's a smear of dirt on my slippers.

The Soldier

Such fine slippers to be used up so quick. The old King showed me them, first thing he did. Said nothing, just led me to a coffer full of the things. The leather soles were quite worn through, but the gold and silver thread on top caught at the light.

The cream-faced footlings hadn't wanted to let me in. Took one look at my boots, that had the clay of the road still on them – though I'd spent a good hour scraping in the yard – took one look at my boots and shook their heads. Be off with you, beggar, one said, waving his dainty fingers like he was brushing a crumb off his livery, what good are you? Go on back to the wars.

But I'd had enough of the wars, to and fro, to and fro, the long spiny grass of the bogs for my bed and a damp ache in my bones I will die with. All for a patch of earth that would never be mine, that I didn't give a toss for, against men who started up from the hills like spirits, or who came behind you with a dagger for your calf and the villages hovels with sour meat and skinny pale-eyed women who smiled and took your pay and would cut your throat in the night, like as not, cold and prone like the land itself.

I killed a man. I killed many, but it's that one face I see, morning and evening, running across the wheat, his boy behind him. The blood gurgled up in his mouth like he was trying to talk. The redness of it, with all that yellow harvest around him and his hair too, yellow like the wheat. I cleaned my blade over and over, but a kind of screaming stirred beneath my skin. I carried it in me day and night, walking, fighting, playing dice, it didn't matter. There it was. Even if I sniffed after whisky till the stars danced and my head was blasted, it was there. And so I took my pay and I left. I am still young, but the whole world is stale and old within me.

For months I walked, picking up a bit of work here and there, not resting, giving away all that I could spare, so that the weariness I carried lay less heavy on me. I dreamed of thinning away to air.

After I shared my meal with her, the old woman stroked my hand and nodded and I felt the warmth of the sun on my face. How long had it been since the sun had licked me fondly? She sat with me for hours on the bank and told me the secrets of the people who passed us on the road.

The younger princesses smiled to see a ragamuffin soldier for their watchman. 'Must we tolerate this?' one said, 'Are there no more noblemen left in all the world, must we be civil to an oaf? Sit him on the little couch, make him bunch up like a monkey.'

And so they placed me, with much laughter, in an alcove. All I could see was the slippers ranged for morning. Beyond the screen their voices were fine as siltless running water. I thought of holding one of those wrought slippers and feeling the silk on my cheek and the cut that a jewel can make. Perhaps at dawn, if I failed, I would break one of their pretty white necks before I lost my own.

Then the eldest came around the screen to me and she did not laugh. She offered me the wine sadly, so that I almost drank it to cheer her. She took my hands between her own and bent her head a moment. She looked up haughty enough then, but her eyes met mine.

The Eldest Princess

His gaze unnerves me. I take his hands between my own. So rough! When I bend my head they smell of sweat and earth. I think of the prince who waits for me on the lake, with his clean skin. Sometimes I make him blonde and sometimes dark, it makes no difference. I cannot bear to watch the soldier drink. There have been so many! It is not we who called for their deaths, it's a bargain they make freely with my father. My hands have no blood on them. But the strange, ragged man sees into my eyes.

Every night I open the door. So many nights and each one the same. Immediately the scents of the gardens caress us, sweet and pure, flowers of air and emeralds. I part the gold and silver branches that hang like lace over the path and we step down, my sisters and I, to where our princes wait to row us under the moon.

Oh, the dark silent water and then the dazzle of the dance, with the bright lights whirling and the soft brush of a new partner's lips as he hints of love and desire, and the dresses all new and the tables decked with dainties. All I have thought to dream of. Night after night. Our pretty slippers, quite worn through. And in the morning what emptiness I feel.

I have taken to walking alone through the afternoons, among the beeches and the silver birches in the park. I listen to the birds but I know they do not sing for me. They sing of summer, of territory and desire. Shades of green sway around me and sometimes the yellow sun shines through and the dead leaves are golden and then brown beneath my boots.

I put by my slippers and I turn to watch him wake. He stretches the sleep from his limbs. First one arm and then the other, his whole body reaching into air. We are summoned as usual to watch the judgement upon him.

Has something broken, or has it been released? When he stands before my father and produces the gold and the silver branches I could slap him for his grin of triumph. What can he know of dancing? Then he looks right at me. Yes, I am tired of foxtrots and quadrilles, of waltzes and galliards. Yes.

I will take him by the hand and lie down beneath the beeches and the birdsong. His body will press me into the soil and I will breathe the sharp tang of the fallen leaves and look up into the green and blue above.

Eleanor Porter

I have always had a soft spot for a monster.
Hirsute, saturnine and ugly
as long as, beneath the hair, there beats
a wounded and a lonely heart.

The beauty of the beast lies in his soft spot,
his yearning apprehension of loveliness
his exposed flesh,
and his need to be loved.
Maybe we all know about that.

But Grendel is different.
Grendel carries the mark of Cain
and has a murderer's heart.
He devours as he lives, a shape-shifting
stranger to warmth and to embrace.

Was he enraged by the sound of fellowship,
echoing from the mead-hall,
or simply driven mad by noise?
To my mind there's a world of difference.

And then he made a mistake, a bad one as it happens.
He picked the wrong man.
This was never going to end well.

At least he had a mother who loved him.
She loved him with a devouring, demonic fervour
that shadowed her own death and shrieked through the halls.
But the revenge-price was too high
the blood too black
and the sword too strong.

No, a soft spot for this monster would be wrong

Diana Cant

Beyond the stream
a Cherry Blossom bends
into a fitful beckoning
as if some reflex
tensioned sinew
in its wood
and twisted gestures
from it.

She would not
have crossed the water there.
Narrow, yes, but fast and deep;
its steep banks
slippery with green.
But they persisted.
Made the meadow.
Moved like molluscs
through the matted grass.
Every step compressed
their flattened wake
the thin rain silvered
to a cobwebbed thread.

She watched their incremental
contours ratchet up,
complicate the hillside
with their knot.
Heard the clatter
of their armour
as the mountainside
unravelled them,
strung them out
like washing on a line.

She'd take her time with them.
Become the woman
they could not resist.
(Men rarely see
what they're not looking for).

She greets each one in turn,
placates them with a kiss

then lets them sleep.

No longer shy
she sheds her shape,
they'll understand their fate
when they're awake.

David J. Costello

Joro-Gumo: a creature from Japanese mythology that could shape-shift into a beautiful woman.

Arachsola sighed. She was lonely. All around her were happy couples, holding legs and being all lovey-dovey. It wasn't fair. Her companions assured her that her time would come, 'It had to, because Arachsola is *so* beautiful,' they said.

Looking down at herself, she realised that her friends were telling the truth. That round and voluptuous black shiny belly – with those seductive spots on top and that lovely red hourglass marking underneath. And how about those long legs. Blimey, she was magnificent. But she was still alone.

One day, Arachsola's prayers were answered. She was peckish so she went to check her web. It was empty. She couldn't understand it. Her webs may not have been as pretty as those of her friends, a bit of a mess really, but they were strong and usually productive. That's when she met him.

'That's a great web,' said a deep voice and a black figure shot away and hid under the woodpile.

'Thanks,' said Arachsola, 'Er, do I know you?'

Eight eyes shone from beneath a stick. 'No, I'm new round here.'

'Wow,' thought Arachsola, 'he might be single!'

A black leg poked out from the stick, followed by a black body. 'I'm Arachcena,' he said, and darted under a log.

'Arachsola,' she replied, shaking a little with unaccustomed lust, having just seen most attractive orange joints on her new acquaintance's legs.

'Pleased to meet you, you *Goddess,* you!' said Arachcena, waggling the red and white stripes on his abdomen, before scuttling behind a tree.

'Ooooh!' said Arachsola, preening herself and not caring that Arachcena was half her size.

It was a lovely wedding. The bride blushed and the groom, though small, performed very well. All Arachsola's friends toasted the happy couple with vintage aphid-juice, and danced the tarantella.

***

Surrounded by the remains of the wedding breakfast, Arachsola sighed and suppressed a hiccup and a most unladylike burp.

Alone again. Oh well.

Alison Mordey

She is riding the hound again.

There she is, her thighs welded to its lichened skin; her foot nuzzling its lunar surface, studded with an abandonment of space-ships and satellite debris. Her elegant fingers bridle its iron jaw, as she croons *this way, that way/you will go where I want you to go/you will do whatever I want of you,* while her head…

But no, it is not *her* head, not a woman's head at all. Instead, the moon-struck lip of another animal stretches from the shoulders of the female form, to nestle on the long brow of the beast. Yes, a hare.

'Lady-Hare on Dog' she reads now, on the label belonging to the sculpture, guarding the entrance to the gallery. She had entered the place to escape the rain – nothing more. But now she has seen *this*. A hare, riding a hound. A hare, not her, at all.

Only, it doesn't matter. What she sees is not what is there. But… it doesn't matter. She can make it her own, it *is* her own. She can own it, like this hare owns the beast. Like she did once before.

She touches the cold, cratered flesh, nerves taut for the whine of an alarm, the rushing of clipped heels. But there is nothing. Of course, she cannot hurt it, nothing can hurt it. She can't score it with a knife, as some have done to paintings far greater than those that hang here. Nor can she hurl and smash it, as she could the lord-and-lady figurines ornamenting the upper floor. The sculpture is an earth-bound giant. She leans her weight into it, an eye catching the red winking eye she now spots above her. But still no-one comes; and nothing moves. Bronze, she reads. Cast bronze, with the detritus of human life thrown in (that seeming space debris made from scraps of toys, machinery) – the sculptor's life. Hers.

She picks up the information sheet accompanying the piece, and begins to read… reads how the sculptor's first hares were offered at her feet by her proud, tail-thumping dogs. Spirits broken, as surely as the crooked necks; strong hearts stilled at last.

She has been like that. Once upon a time, she was the hunted hare, always running, always scared, deserving the mocking names from the poet's litany. She was *white-face/hugging the ground/sitting tight, bearing men's scorn.* Yes, she took it all. Or… she was the cauldron-stirring servant-boy changing into a hare, to be outdone/run by the mother/magician/greyhound. The trembling creature, cowering under the Saint's gown, in flight from the Prince and his tall riders. The witch, bleeding and breathless, shutting the door on the jeering farmers so close behind. These were the tales her grandmother told her – the abject hare, the beaten hare, its luckless names recited by the hunter, a charm for his power. *Her* names, recited by the man, to keep her in *his* power. And... slut. Bitch. Mine... while he cut off her golden curls (his own charm). Mine... as her body wilted into submission. Mine... as he.... Mine.

She took it all.

And still should take it after he was caught.

'It's better this way,' they told her. The men in suits and uniforms, the clucking women. 'Otherwise, you will have to go through it all again, you will be torn apart again. It's not worth it.'

But there were other tales for the hare, she knew. Picture-book, nursery-rhymed, the sleeping hunter, the sneaking hare, the rifle in his hands. *Run, man, run/My turn to have some fun.* Tables turned.

And she followed the pages of the papal Decretals, her fingers tracing the archer-hare, as it fired arrow after arrow into the start-eyed hound, as it whipped the carriage of the chained captive towards the waiting gallows, as it stood and sniggered as the creature met its doom. The story reversed.

Reversal... because the hare is a shape-shifter, it doesn't have to stay as it is, it can transform into something quite different. The moon, the corn, the Rabbit, the cat. The witch, the Queen, the Spring, the Dawn.

Just as the sculptor turned the bundled scraps of blood and fur into these bronze and wire monsters, hybrids of form and meaning, metaphors of female mythic strength.

Just as there are other names for the hare. *Starer* – as she sat in the courtroom, and lifted her face, and looked straight at him. *Scare-the-man.* As she kept her voice strong when she told what he had done, and saw his body shake and his skin blanch.

And *flame-leaper*, as the burning shame was fired at her, then repeated by the baying (press) pack closing in; but she did not flinch.

And so she defeated the predator, the man.

She reaches up to stroke the lady-hare. The hare-lady. Her. The woman.

She places her hand over the hare/hand.

She is in charge of the beast, in control, facing forward. Her grown-back golden hair/hare's golden ears is/are long and proud, flowing behind her/it. She is victim no more.

Diana Powell

If there's a lover, husband asleep in bed or aching
with questions – he's hidden off-canvas,

as the younger child wriggles from his mother's arms to join
the hound on the left of his sister who's one step

behind. Hound might have been the one to save them
with stereo smell, polyphonic hearing, wolverine jaw –

but tell me, who isn't walking in the dark these days
when what begins as a stroll of good intentions becomes

a fleeing to nowhere in a mess of blue, paint slapped on,
blind, reckless: cerulean, saxe, prussian, cobalt

turned glaucous with too much haste, hesitation … too much
rubbing off, blurring the edges until the weather breaks, the path

ends, the only foothold a slice of air, a dulled sea of failed
approaches, no door

leading to another, primer already primed to erase them.
They are nothing but ghosts swimming for their lives,

stretching out their arms, holding onto their hearts,
having set out with the light before them,

fruit in their pockets,
wind in the trees.

Linda Rose Parkes

An ugly thought crept into my head today.
I don't know whose it was, it certainly wasn't mine.
'Kill her' it said. And it was quite a slight insult –
'Your hair – do you dye it?' she'd asked.

As the nasty thought elbowed itself to the front
of my head, I noticed it had fat thighs, a bit
like mine – thin lips like Sister Octavia –
small eyes like Lenin. It battered my lovely thoughts
which were too polite to make a fuss – those about
autumn leaves and garden shrubs.

It always happens when I've had a bath, when I'm
clean and pure. That's when the wicked thought
slithers in – gets its foot in the door, flops down,
makes itself at home, brews itself a pot of tea.

Then it gets at me,
tells me my sweet thoughts are fakes –
whispers in my voice – makes the same small
grammatical mistakes.

Angela Cooke

Tree Down

For years you blindsided me,
stole my light,
in the blink of an eye
turned into a tower,
a conical darkness that made space
for nests, withstood all winds,
at night, you threw in your lot
with other shadows.

You had to go.
Expertly dismembered,
branches falling and fanning out,
a messy mosaic.
They stopped short of your roots:
majesty reduced to a stump.

Who would have thought ?
I miss you,
steadfast shadow that had me believing
that some things last for ever.
I have lost my cover,
in seeing, I am seen.

Jacqueline Sousa

THE CHILD   came up to me and whispered low
'my balloon has the universe
inside, just for me'
I agreed that was marvellous
a wonder indeed
that he could hold
a string
that held a universe

He sensed I was not
totally sincere
just humouring him
the set of my mouth,
the giggle in my eyes
told him of disbelief and
a patronising attitude

he said again
'the universe is in it!
not foolin' or joking
it scares me sometimes
that I might let it go
who knows who might grab
the universe in their hands
bad hands, careless hands'

I began to sweat
not from belief
but from a possibility that he
believed
in a way that twisted
tormented his mind with the string
held tight in a small hand
while the eyes stared in fear

'what if I brush a pin,
a thorn
and it pops
what happens to us?
with a universe exploding in our faces?
will the universe expand
out there
in space?
will there be room
for the world...
and us?'

I thought and said
'if you have the universe contained
then we're in there too
and all the popping will do
is put the universe into the universe
because we're in there
and out here
all at the same time'

he looked so thoughtful
and I could see the idea
working its way through
and the child who barely
reached up to my waist
understood
worked it out
agreed

he reached for a rose
growing nearby just there
and broke off a thorn
and studied it well
before he looked at me
once again
'I hope you're right'

Glen Proctor

A CASE OF RELATIVITY

The sun was sinking in the sea
Or so it seemed to you and me
Although, in actuality
The sinking was illusory
A case of relativity
(The earth was spinning backwardly)
Thus spoke the bloke, the very same
Who then went on to make the claim
That our mistake should cause no shame
No matter! We could always blame
The limits of our reference frame.
He smiled and left the way he came
He never gave his name

Mike O'Brien

One day, we will get ahead of ourselves
and stand, arms outstretched, where water lips the
land, waiting for our wave to come to shore.

Out at sea, wherever weather comes from,
wind inspires a wave, energy rises,
gravity pulls water back, down and flat,
round and rolling: the sea circles itself,
whilst our wave pushes past, riding oceans.

Between maps, though cities sprawl, there is no
constant but collapse, nothing abides and
shouting at the tides will not turn them back.

Beyond the beach, black rocks stand sentinel
and mark a passing, their shadows reaching
back towards the land, as the sun rises.

We do not need to travel fast, but wish
for wind to make us last, and to sustain
us: as the sea is brim and wide with waves
that thin their influence into water.

In sight of land waves rise in panic to
grasp at water, bubble air and break the
shore, but we know that it has weathered more.

One day, we will get ahead of ourselves
and stand, arms outstretched, where water lips the
land, and our wave will run gently, becoming
capillary: relax into the shore.

Scott Butterworth

Float

Winter's roar on a frosty night
would find me sitting on the sill,
in an old cotton dressing gown,
lights off.
I would throw open the bedroom window
and listen to the sounds of the sea,
with the path of moonlight
paving the way a dream might take.

Go to sleep.
The door shifted and
I'd jump between winceyette sheets
as mother's arm eased the window closed.
She warned me of sirens
who make men weak
and mermaids who drown
the meek and good
unless you say your prayers.

Through the glass, the physics of
a wave's increasing asymmetry
transferred energy as sound.
How shifting gravity as the moon
waxes and wanes creates tides.

Scatter my ashes in the ocean,
let my atoms drift across the
wide, life-giving sea and maybe
I will feel fingers ripple through
amniotic fluid.
Hear new waves.

Clint Wastling

This beach is never blank.
In spite of the wind's whip and the swipe of the waves
it lies under sky like an open page,
its ridged lines written by the tide
as though the moon has pressed her frowning forehead to the sand.

Here bladderwrack spells out darkly
in gothic script the water-logged names of the sea;
and the dot-dash of cockle and razor shell
encoding a secret, safe and salty;
the pattern of runes printed by sea-birds' feet, untranslatable.

We and our shadows walk the shore.
Yours is short and never still. Mine,
a measure of my days, stretches long to the West.
Seabirds, circling, freckle the sand with shade.
I throw my arms wide, hair a halo in the east wind,

and you begin to draw
with your spade around the shape my shadow makes.
The plastic blade slices wet sand. Your small hand
cannot hold the line, swerving out of true.
You make a botch of me. We laugh, and race towards the sea.

And this is what the years will do.
Some time distant you will half-recall the day,
the beach whose mysteries you pondered; and someone –
outline wavering, face no longer clear –
sketched in sand between one tide and the next.

Susan Wallace

Grandchildren, hot and tired,
are flopped in deck-chairs;
it's tea-time soon, so spades, rugs, wind-break
go back in the beach hut.
Foot washing, de-sanding,
the steep trudge up the cliff
from where, looking back,
the beach reveals its patterns:
the birth and death of waves,
a flock of sand pools
that have drained each into each
as the tide ebbs;
and where grandfather, a tiny figure,
is still industriously damming and digging,
lost in the sand-child he used to be.

John Gilham

Once I was beautiful
A rose among thorns,
A pale Asian with African hair,
That's me posing for Modigliani.
That's me with Jacob Boehme.
That's me behind The Maid of Orleans.
In the sea, in the endless sea,
Dead from typhoid, murdered by Empires or Spanish Flu, the ravages of
war, consumption.
Do you see me? Worshipping the Greek Gods, the Norse Gods,
Praying to The Son Of Man?
I have knelt in all their holy places.
Sing me any hymn in any tongue;
I know them all.
I am The Boer, The Troubadour, The Carthaginian, A Flower Girl, Soul
Queen Of Harlem.
Come, comb my hair with scented seashells, fill me with sweetcorn and
rainbow trout. Bless this Now.
My skin is crusted with salt: from The Baltic, The Atlantic, The Red Sea,
Dead Sea, The Caribbean.
The waves tear down temples and cover cities and the sea remembers all.
I am grateful to live for this one perfect moment.
For I heard Parmenides ask,
"If the past runs dark with sorrow
that strikes blind the hour's watchman,
how will we see tomorrow
if it's night where our days have ran?"
And though there are those unawakened
whose world is yet lived in narrow streets
with doors marked 'them' and 'me', they too, in time, will know
the still and endless sea.

Mike McNamara

109

Our intestines are 27 feet long,
contain 900 folds and if laid out flat could
cover an entire tennis court,
mulch a dozen good sized holly bushes,
velum the complete works of William Shakespeare,
upholster rows 12 to 18 of a Boeing 737,
yellowbox the Old Kent Road,
plait 870 scoobidoos,
eyepatch a sloop of pirates,
wrap'n twist 6,000 Murray mints,
straphandle three carriages of commuters,
hosepipe a modest house fire,
strop a year's worth of cut-throat razors,
cup and saucer 2,000 toy tea sets,
innertube a fleet of bicycles,
garter the Morris men of West Riding,
greaseproof 800 upside-down cakes,
wetwipe 200 toddlers' bottoms,
skingraft a herd of elephants,
ropestraddle the Cheddar Gorge,
releaf a single blasted oak,
 or digest your food –
the career path of choice.

Claire Booker

resting in darkness
rich, dull gleam unseen
          unclaimed and
                    waiting for
                              release, for
                              daylight, for
me.

Greetings, beloved
I am the widow of a man
whose name you may not know
but who was very rich

                    the dreams of avarice are
                    limitless, like those of
                    falling, or of catching trains

His many, many millions
are all in gold, but sadly inaccessible
to me; I need your help,
for which I shall pay well

                              the blinding light of Africa
                                   the dust that blows
                                        into my eyes
                                             the loa loa
                    none of this prevents the sight
                    of ingots, neatly piled,
              and I can hear their solid clunk
                         each heavy bar against the next

Please help me; give
the details of your bank account,
and I shall send those millions
to you straightaway.

                    and now, as if I've stumbled
                         on a golden nightjar's nest
                              at dusk   and up
                              it flies   a clatter
                         of affronted wings
                    my greed-dream shatters

111

and I fall to earth
and quickly click on "junk mail"
and move on

Peter J King

He shows, she follows –
now bird, now flower.
'Dancing is poetry with arms and legs,'
said Baudelaire.
At such a time all barriers are down
and *everything* feels like poetry.

Mambo is Congolese for
'Conversation with the Gods'.
It's like playing a new tune
on an old instrument – steps complicated,
the rhythm, possibility.
Challenge. Promise.

They're perfect together.
She's as good as her teacher –
instinctive and joyfully open
to the unknown.
There's the sense of order and release,
each dance a stanza.

Sally Festing

Four arthritic knees, two stiff backs,
in a slow ambling ordeal down Main St.
Casual words about each shop window,
entering many, poking around,
can't find anything to buy.
They stop for coffee to rest their pains.
Surprised, alarmed at growing old.
One mind formed from motorbikes and mountain climbing,
rowdy drinking, wildness still around his iron-gray head,
shadowed by dead friends.
The other, bald, from Benedictine monasteries,
plainchant, cloisters, football,
discipline held his hand and heart.
As they sit among the sounds of coffee making
and youngsters tapping at their screens,
the wild man says,
'Night has come over the Atlantic.
Can you see the chaotic mounds of thrashing water?'
It was a game they played each week.
'I can,' says the priestly friend. 'An all-directions storm,
deep-muscled waves slamming across each other,
like those soldiers fighting in the dark.'
'Ships are tossed about and swallowed in the deep.'
'Fish and whales, shoulders hunched in fear,
are thrown around like dead leaves in the wind.'
'And snow tumbles onto the towering surges.'
'Yes, I see snow falling into the dark ocean.'
Next door an antiques shop to pick through,
and after another half hour
the tottering *flâneurs* will find
a pub and pint to finish.

Kieran Egan

There is quite a bit here
I do not understand
Or think I do but don't

Try these for starters:
Steiner's Nietzchean insistence
Acts of commentary can become acts of art

I mean, I ask you, and I wonder if it should be Art
Or ART even
The big 'A'

Then throw in more philosophy talk, so we really know our place:
Wittgentstein's concept of language games
Wittgentstein's – I just like saying this – *paratactic aphoristic style*

Wow. But wait, it gets better:
Apodictic certainties
Gotcha

But, my favourite:
Hierophantic cadences
I think I get this

And, to finish:
Exultant antagonism
To do with poetry v thought

I buy that
I will sing it
My own cadenza.

Tony McCabe

Come out, you cow! I know you're in there,
whimpering in your stinking cave.
I've tried flattery, which gets me nowhere,
tried winkling you out with a wet ear-poke –
metaphorically speaking. Shouted out
some of your past winning lines.

Grunt, Muse! Groan, shriek, stammer!
Anything but whimper like that.
I can do nothing with whimpering,
there's no bloody market for it.
I need a starter, a bit of kindling!
I try shouting, 'Sing, Muse,'
– there's nothing but silence,
as though you'd left the building.
Tried "rosy-fingered" or "wine-dark,"
but it's like kicking a motorbike
that's out of fuel.

Exasperated –
against all that's holy –
I rush the cave entrance,
force myself past the briars and boulders,
scour its passages and chambers.
Of course, you aren't there.
Of course, no sign of habitation, ever.
Of course, the whimpering is mine.

Kieran Egan

My blood spills out from split skin
Like a pomegranate bursting on its tree,
With pleasing nectar sucked by junky wasps.

Alarm! Alarm! Let not the sharks nor crawling ants know
No! nor neither flying things that long to lay foul maggots in
This rich delectable food.

My blood flows – trickling in the waxy furrows
Of my skin – the skin that has betrayed me
– Not held it in.

My blood with pulses redly drips.
The captains and the corporals scramble.
Regiments of platelets and anti-bodies

With congealant agencies spring to action.
The liquid slows, thickens and stops.
Invisible sappers and sealers swarm

To the wound and patch and sew
And mend as best they can.
I wear proudly my scab, look forward to the scar

– Memento of my skirmish with this hard and jagged world:
The ravishment from which my juicy flesh
Must ever shrink.

Clive Donovan

The thought of the butchery of her body wounds her bravery.
She already mourns her soft hair.
She's pained by a scar
that will cut her in two,
and my heart winces
for this tampering with her beauty.

But I want want want that scar!
I want the raised evidence
that the tumour has gone,
I will love that scar dearly,
caress it daily,
devote myself
to its ugly beauty.

We are in dangerous territory here.
We tread softly towards the brink,
not too near, she tilts her head,
If we were to find ourselves there ...
she says,
If the op went wrong ...
The policies ...
Just so you know ...
And I search her eyes
And if, My Angel, ...

How would I bury you?

Lizzie Holden

Looking for the rain I climbed
from drought dry onto arid hill.
Sky greeted me, hot empty, blue
reflecting in scoured quartz.
A thousand feet below, churning dust
mocked lost cloud inversions.

I descended, let the hill guide my feet
until, stumbling, I kicked out a rock.
Water oozed: foolishly I kicked again.
Flood threw me aside. When I stood,
all dust was gone, the glen's detritus
carved into intricate braids
like the map of a life scalpels
scarred into your saved flesh.

Grahaeme Barrasford Young

CURTAINS   They try to clamor in her living room
but a) it's vacant: who would hear but her?
and b) they can but whisper like the steam
that coils and rises from the radiator,

more a sigh, a half-hiss, than a scream,
or signal to be filled with meaning later.

Don't misconstrue the loneliness for gloom,
however. They've such memories of when
the brass pot overflowed with rex begonia,
caladium, once a philodendron

that lived for years till a bout of pneumonia
kept her from watering it. The eldest son,

who lives just down the road, has brought
her every winter, for the window pot,
some seasonal thing, poinsettias usually,
two or three times a miniature Christmas tree

live, from a box, mail order. Since she had
to water it, she would. But she'd grow sad

when the needles started turning brown and yellow.
She reared him to be considerate, though,
and this season she asked him bluntly not
to buy a plant at all. He asked her why.

She either heard and didn't want to tell,
or didn't hear. She can't hear very well

anymore. The curtains sway as if to sigh,
or to remind him of the years she tried
to keep things growing—when she couldn't, lied—
and of all of the poinsettias that have died.

He's filled the pot nonetheless, too dutiful
not to. She adjusts the curtains and whispers,
Beautiful.

James B. Nicola

My mother's things, there are so few of them,
She'd always chuck things in the bin if there
Was just a hint that they were making up
Their minds to irritate. 'No bloody good,'
She'd say, accusingly, and anything
And everything would go. Not one trace left
That I was once a child. All gone: my toys,
My books, my Sheffield Wednesday scarf, my soft
Brown monkey that I used to take to bed.
All her stuff's gone as well. Just one tin box
For life insurance policies and snaps
And birth and death certificates and two
St Margaret's parish magazines. One with
My christening, one with my father's death.
Her life stripped down to what she thought it meant.
Not much, I seem to hear her say, Not much.

Alan Smith

I'M SORRY

I let you drop
into the ground,
that dark place.
Your bones in a box
kept from me
by the soil
they insisted
must lie between us.

Your skin has flaked into the earth
but maybe your bones
might shine
if I came to you,
brushed them clean,
stroked them and stroked them
until they gleamed.

I don't mind the soil,
any love that has leached
I will replace.

And you?

Do you miss your bones?
Do you secretly wish you could slip down
to join them again,
fit round them again,
walk with them
as I so long to do?

Lizzie Holden

sat there   as when she died
staring at the table

as were he aware   of the weight of it
the silence   settling into the earth

to seep deeper in   among the leaves
the last stones

of his own weight   waiting there

as if there were words to be heard
sounds to stir the sense of them

to set there
to inscribe the child's name
to write the terrible cry

Ray Malone

Patting your pockets with an officious
politeness you would have admired,
was the last time I touched you;
following an enquiry as to whether
personal artefacts were about you.

I had no idea what was about you.
I was beside your stillness. A stillness like
Nannie and Grandad's house when they
were on holiday: their house devoid
of laughter and pre-feast steam was a shell.

I would wait for its reanimation by
sticky plastic and sharp-strawed gifts,
a slideshow of mahogany skin
and places with greenhouse air:
now the empty house of you was lying there.

My hands were much too tentative and soft
to give purpose to my task
and my efforts felt inconsequential
and blurred; I wanted to touch you
and felt that I needed a reason

to steer me decently through the reality
of being alongside the shell of you.
I had held your warm, blood-coursed hand
when I had left that afternoon
and I hoped that living touch had said

what I wanted it to say, as my hands skimmed
the outside of your pockets and paramedics
looked politely and sombrely on.
My task was a shadow motive,
focussing the struggle against feeling you gone.

Damon Young

When she had gone, their faces remained as masks of mockery;
painted, pouting lips and long-fringed lashes,
glass-eyed through glass.
Shelved cabinets shivering by footfall
stirred them to whispering witness
of all their unseeing eyes had seen.

Fifty when the first
graven image fawned upon her fancy,
she had found a way to recapture her youth.
Restore, recreate, resurrect discarded dolls;
remake them in her own image.

Fidgety fingers found purpose in perfection of face and fashion,
hair restyled in the many incarnations of her own.
Lynda in her prime lived again, plastic made almost-flesh
by one succumbing fast to vagaries of time and trial.

Then disease and decay.

Masks of mockery, they gazed unflinching
as the cancer ate her from within.
No hand could repaint the fading face,
no fingers re-root the chemo-bald scalp.

When she had gone, their faces remained as masks of mockery.
Daily, they taunted the one who had loved her
in spite of all flaws besetting the flesh.
Raging, he took a hammer to their glazed immortality,
and toppled them from their pedestals of endless youth and pleasure.

Yvonne Hendrie

Cap   Noose   Pin   Lever   Drop

Cap... It was in part a calling, my craft.
I was put on Earth to do it. My father
told me, aged eleven, that one day
I'd become the 'Official Executioner'.
My mission, my one-man expedition
passed down from him to me. I thought
it just the job for me: travel, adventure,
death, romance. Like poor Uncle Johnny
whistling his way to the barbed wire fence.
Even my teacher smiled when I replied
to that old question: "What do you want
to be when you grow up?" Well, it was
either that or work with horses.

Noose... Father told me some stories:
his training days getting a nose for the craft.
Tightening the noose on sandbag dummies.
Calculating and recalculating the drop,
their crudely stitched faces grinning all
the way down (someone's idea of a joke.)

Pin... He kept a diary of executions: a thick
black tome – The Grim Reaper of books, like
a family Bible. He entered each detail piously:
name, age, height, weight, condition of neck.
It was a science to him but he remembered
them all, knowing it was he who always
looked them last in the eyes.

Lever... Each journey to the scaffold was
singular: the painful comedy of a man
complaining about the tightness of the rope.
The pathos of another who was allowed
to smoke, his cigarette still held between
his lips when they cut him down.

Drop... Now I carry the tools of this trade:
rope, rule, wire, shackle, measure, pliers, cap.
My calf-leather wrist-strap, reserved for
special cases, torn eyehole-to-eyehole by
the rage of a German spy.

Cap   Noose   Pin   Lever   Drop

There's a rhythm to this business. You have
to get it right to avoid any unnecessary
stress. It's no different for a woman, except,
for decency we adjust the leg-strap. They
are always braver than men. But I treated
them all the same. Even The Beast of Belsen:
"Schnell, schnell... Make it quick!"
I always did. Knot under left jaw for a clean
break. Swift end. Respect in death.

Ellis went without a last word, despite what
the papers said. Let them print their tangled
lies. The last woman I will hang. *Cap... Noose...
Pin...* My ambition's fading. Executions solve
nothing. *Lever... Drop...* nothing.

Did I tell you she never spoke a word?

Natalie Scott

*Albert Pierrepoint hanged 433 men and 17 women in his career,
including Ruth Ellis, executed at Holloway Prison on 13th July 1955. He
resigned his post on 23rd February 1956.*

*(i.m. Emily 'Mickey'
Hahn, 1905 - 1997,
writer and traveller
extraordinaire
whose granddaughter
delivered the eulogy at
her funeral)*

If all grandmothers are golden
mine was a self-generating
combustion engine of a meteor
lapping up the world and its offerings
as a cat slurps cream.

A trip to the zoo?
She whooped heartfelt news clips
LOUDLY in front of the gibbons' cage,
a language she no doubt learned
when living with pygmies and
slow-footing it across Africa
(which is how come I can swear
fairly fluently in Swahili).

Other grandmothers might hang
long, invisible 'No Smoking' banners
from the tips of their twitching noses
to their front doors; mine smoked cigars,
a sedate indulgence given a determined
two years of smoking opium in Shanghai
I always wanted to be an addict.
She kicked the habit, travelled on,
but in later years had a soft spot
for younger relatives, would loan out
her flat for wild parties and not turn
a grey hair at a whiff of pot.

Years of books and newspaper articles
sent from the four corners catalogued her life.
Only one poem was published (despite
an affair with a poet during the opium years)
a few months before she died.
I guess she'd been too busy living
her ninety-two years. *Books you can
write anywhere – one step, then another,
post it off.* With poems she'd need to sit
and think. Not grandma's style.

Her life was a global Catherine wheel
of experiences, her mantra
No-one said not *to go.*
It never crossed anyone's mind.

Patricia Leighton

CHILDREN

At first they are all ours,
Mini-Me Mini-You,
Our breath and our kisses.
To them, we possess the ultimate power –
To shoo away dragons from dark recesses.

Then school beckons,
And the bonds loosen.
New friends
New skills
New tests
New spills.

After which,
Secondary education
Sees them orbit
Far beyond parental limits,
Widening scope, shunning reason,
Until at the ancient age
Of fifteen, they rage
And break free.

Now we are the fascist Old Guard,
Divorced from their ultra-left.
They are the new communards.

*   *   *

The lane shakes out summer.
Girls, pomegranate-sated, stall
And hover suggestively.
And old men shrink away,
Haunted by the curlew's call.

Youth and age,
Sense, nonsense;
And all the while
We watch helpless,
The final point of reference.

Michael Newman

Vinyl memories
your songs engraved
across my poetry

Jane Stuart

Flights of Fancy: *Circling the Sun* by Paula McLain
Virago
ISBN 978-1-84408-830-0 pp 414 £14.99

Birthday in August? How do you plan to spend it? How would you spend it if it was your 79th? Naomi Christie, ex-president of the British Women Pilots' Association, spent hers standing on a Tiger Moth – in flight! That was on 4th August 1990. But the fame and success of women in aviation goes back way beyond that.

If *Circling the Sun,* Paula McLain's recent book, is a mixture of genres – history, memoir, fiction – it's surely appropriate. After all, **Beryl Markham**, protagonist of the book, was an adventurer, horse trainer, pilot, writer, and romantic – a heroine for every taste.

It's more than eighty years since the disappearance of American pilot Amelia Earhart, the first woman to fly solo across the Atlantic. Her name is familiar, and we salute her bravery, determination and success.

But let's fly the flag (the Union Jack, this time) for Beryl Markham, the first woman – British – to fly the Atlantic solo from *east* to *west.* The prevailing Atlantic winds make a westbound flight more hazardous, requiring more time, fuel and pilot endurance, yet on 4th September 1936, Markham took off from Abingdon, England, to fly the 3,400 miles to New York.

In fact, she crash-landed on Cape Breton Island, Nova Scotia, some 700 miles short of her goal, due to fuel starvation caused by icing of the fuel tank vents on her Vega Gull plane, *The Messenger.* Nevertheless, she was awarded the title of pioneer aviator as the first woman to achieve the westward Atlantic flight.

Flying wasn't Markham's only achievement. She was born in England, but her father bought a farm in the Kenyan Rift Valley and her family relocated when she was four years old. Her colourful Kenyan childhood and youth furnished her with a love and understanding of African tribal culture and of animals in general. Author McLain implies that Markham's huge capacity for survival and adapting to adverse circumstances might have been due, partly, to her mother's abandoning her when she was only six. No need, she implies, for us to be defined by our adverse circumstances.

At sixteen, Markham was married (note the passive voice) to another farmer, but that marriage hardly left the starting blocks. There followed two more marriages including the birth of a son, Gervaise, to Markham and her second husband, Mansfield Markham, and many love affairs.

Among them may have been an all-encompassing devotion to Denys Finch Hatton, who played a part in Markham's early aviation lessons. She appeared briefly in the 1985 film *Out of Africa,* as wild, feisty, horse-loving Felicity.

But to Markham belong a string of firsts: as well as her flying achievements, she was the first woman, while still in her teens, to earn a race-horse trainer's license and to chalk up a number of winners. She pioneered the practice, as a bush pilot, of scouting herds of elephant from the air.

She was pinned down and bitten by a lion, needing stitches the length of her leg, but when that lion was caught and caged, she felt a pang of guilt and sorrow for him: *Killing is what he's meant to do.*

Paula McLain writes with compassion but without judgement, leaving that to the reader. Her prose is dazzlingly beautiful and precise. History, she says, is boring; but her passion for biography, the story of lives rather than the dates of battles, is what drives her to do her research so meticulously.

McLain was privileged to travel to Kenya and visit the places that Markham frequented – Nairobi, her father's farm, the Muthaiga Club – venue for colonialists' parties. She even visited Finch Hatton's grave. She testifies to an intimate connection with Markham: both were abandoned by their mothers, then reunited decades later; both were brought up with horses; both married young to considerably older husbands.

Markham's life was punctuated by scandal, hardship and poverty, but far from capitulating to difficulties, playing the victim or succumbing to self-pity, she treated life's hard knocks as stepping stones to strength, independence and adventure. Not, it seems, unlike McLain herself.

Helen Parker

Fermata: *'Foothold'* by Pam Zinnemann-Hope
Ward Wood Publishing
ISBN 978-1-908742-65-0 pp 76 £9.99

Music is time perfectly expressed. A single sound is a note, a pulse is a moment; the one cannot exist without the other. In her first collection of poetry, Pam Zinnemann-Hope celebrates this connection and its most unexpected forms.

Opening the collection and quoted in full, Thomas Hardy's poem 'In a Museum' asks us to consider the unfathomable: time as a loop, in which unnamed birdsong connects past and present and becomes part of the music of the universe. The antithesis of this, 'They Tell Us It Will Come Tonight' describes the "certain hush", the definite "rest" we sense before a fall of snow; from a collective chorus to absolute silence; from unimaginable concept to intimate moment.

'Foothold' presents physical and psychological barriers. Some are legendary, 'Eurydice', others are personal: small but significant impediments, as in the sequence 'Distances'. The poet's husband is a composer and in 'Distances I' Pam describes him writing music as though he were marking a map to a new world, one which she cannot read. In 'Distances II' she is invited to listen to the resulting piece, but the border is still between them:

"I'm sitting in the old feeding chair
with the tree of life cushion:

I'm watching you stand:
    you like to stand;"

Zinnemann-Hope examines the culture of music with wry affection. She hears it in the playful innocence of her dog playing with a ball and a stick, '3 Liszt Etudes', and recognises its absurdities in 'The Musicologist and the Birdwatcher', in which two men attempt to capture a lark's unconscious improvisation:

"...when they get home, they slow
the recording they've made;
they slow it, they play it backwards.
Quickly the musicologist annotates.
Now he plays six bars of Beethoven.

Identical, he says,
the camera panning the score.
...
If I had my way
I'd make a sequel
...
about how Beethoven's soul
had entered the lark, backwards;
how it's speeded up."

For Zinnemann-Hope music and nature cannot be separated. Both must be experienced within time, neither can be possessed, except in the memory. In 'Hooke Woods, in Two Movements', Pam takes a walk with her grandson in spring and summer. Nature's music surrounds them both, but it is a warning, a siren. The one sound mentioned, a wren's call, is like a "tiny silver axe."

As she says,

> "It is not yet in your gift to understand
> there's an inscription here, held in each tree:
> history in rings and in the pattern of its branchings,
> it tells of drought, storms, insect attacks; circumstance."

There are echoes of 'Distances II' here: neither is familiar with the language on display. Although an important skill to learn, perhaps she is suggesting, that for the moment at least, there is a freedom that comes from not being able to understand everything.

Although barriers run everywhere, interestingly it is Hardy's constant presence, fatalist though he was, that breaks them down. His work also showed the permeability, the adaptability life must have if it is to survive and this is reflected in Zinnemann-Hope's finest poems. Both poets make little distinction between sacred and secular. Both see a stonemason's work in particular as both conventionally religious and 'pagan,' (word used advisedly) and for them the spirit of the green man as present as ever. His unpredictability and ultimate control guides the stone-balancer:

> "I can't stop dreaming
> of the life of stones
>
> their pitch and poise
> …
> I listen
> through my fingertips:
>
> hear the exact point
> of friction
> …
> I cradle stone's birth
> and stone's death
>
> for that moment I'm a god
> making a person.
>
> Stone draws breath
> I step back.
>
> Stone pulls its weight
> a displacement of air
>
> in stasis
> stone flies."
> ('The Stone-Balancer's Secret')

and infuses the exquisite 'Crab Apple' in which the tree becomes 'a many-armed god', bringing spring into being with a blackbird's song.

This is the highest point of the year, in which spring is renewal and renewal is faith; inseparable. Nothing more is needed.

Zinnemann-Hope writes of the various incarnations of ancient stones with a unique tenderness. Whether they hold fossils, form walls or shelter lives, she makes them seem alive. To the human eye they represent time on pause, but they change; infinitesimally "unbecoming" and "becoming" with each moment. So they allow us a foothold, while showing us we cannot stay long.

Tanya Parker Nightingale

The Unstill Ones by **Miller Oberman**
Princeton University Press.
ISBN: 9780691176833 pp 79 £14.95

With this collection, Miller Oberman has done something quite remarkable. He has mixed his contemporary works with his translations of Old English poems, whose written forms date back to the 8th, 9th and 10th centuries. It is a bold move. The concept may sound indulgent and potentially confused, yet the resulting body of poetry manages to be coherent, moving and provocative.

The successful integration of the poems stems largely from conversations Oberman stages between his own works and his translations, some as a direct response, others informed by his obvious love of Anglo-Saxon culture. 'The Ruin' (trans) conjures a thriving city, its life, its people and its demise, from "this wall-stone, broken by fate"; Oberman's poem of the same name throws us into a moment of decadent and defiant destruction as a modern city burns. The contemporary 'Wulf and Eadwacer' plays on the opacity of the 10th century poem, and adds to the confusion with lines that conflate the fate of a child and of the poem itself. Tone is carefully married. Both Ruin's are muscular and brash while both Wulf and Eadwacer end with vulnerability and loss, for all the initial humour of the modern work. Other poems speak to our imperfect imaginings of the Anglo-Saxon world: brothers are wolves, poets are semi-religious, living alone in wilderness with fire and rock, and people are vulnerable within an uncompromising but magical natural world. Techniques characteristic of Old English poetry, such as alliteration and compounded terms, add to the commonality of language, yet their use is judicious; they are echoes, not pastiche.

The translated works often include gaps in square brackets, sometimes lines at a time, to show where damage to the original manuscripts has erased the words. This is normal academic practice, but it also alters the readers' experience of the poems. Far from encouraging us to fill in the blanks, Oberman celebrates them, allowing individual words to sing out from the silences. The end of 'The Ruin' captures lost grandeur in this way:

"   [   ] That is a kingly thing
              house [   ]
                    [   ] city [   ]"

In Riddle 82, there are fewer words than spaces, but what there are, are elevated to the biblical. At best, this feels like structured poems melting into free association, while the appearance of the sparse words on the page reflects the themes of silence and loss which so many of the poems deal with. In a couple of contemporary poems, he also plays with spaces within lines, the dislocation clarifying each image and making us aware of our eyes traveling across the page as we travel through the poem.

These are restless, searching poems that all, in some way, explore our experience of constant change. In the title work, the moment lovers come together is made timeless by the erotic slide of tense and language:

always now even before
but it is now again and
we were is-ing all over.

In 'On Trans', Oberman plays gleefully with words beginning with those five letters, including some of his own, though with the more sober intent of showing that "*The process of through is ongoing.*" The simple inclusion of the older texts implies the continual passage of time and things lost because of it; the poems are so carefully positioned, however, that you recognise the familiar in them rather than the alien. In opposition to this celebration of change, Oberman identifies the act of naming and self-definition as a misguided "*desire for stillness, for containment*" 'Night Watch'. In the latter work, naming "horse" denies its powerful reality, while in 'Tabula Rasa' the act of tattooing a man with his place in the world suspends him from it, even as that world continues around him.

This is an ambitious collection which is unafraid to explore universal themes, yet it is saved from being overly academic by also being intensely personal. Oberman's voice is so assured and consistent, whether translating or creating, that it is easy to believe you glimpse him within the characters he draws. His parents, his brother, his lovers and ancestors are here as well, poignantly caught in the same cycles of change and loss. Almost in spite of its ambition and grand themes, this collection remains a very individual statement from a unique poet.

Ann Heath

Submerged lives in depths: *'Hyem'* by Robyn Bolam
Bloodaxe Books
978-1-78037-394-2 pp 70 £9.95

Robyn Bolam's words exert a tidal pressure, gradually drawing you into in a new element; unfamiliar, sometimes cold, but inescapable.

As she says, this current pulls whenever she thinks of home. Be it the Tyne, the hills of Northumberland or her grandparents' misty beginnings in Orkney and Shetland, ideas of home are explored, deconstructed (sometimes literally) and questioned. In 'Where Home Started' home ground itself slips away as, in an early memory, her school bus slides off a bank, heading towards the Tyne. Home is the place from which we set out, and also somewhere we never cease exploring; somewhere we never know entirely.

This sense of macabre mystery is developed in the following poem, 'Changing Sequence', in which the father figure is a "bearded ghost" and the mother is capable of killing:

"Smashing a mouse with a poker against the stone kitchen floor."

Here is another kind of shifting, this time a juggling of memories, in which edges are smoothed:

"So my father will stay a fit, working man, swinging his child onto his chest in the firelight"

In a sense the memories themselves exist in their own element, remade in our minds into something both "dead and fresh."

Familiar landscapes extend into history in 'Basil Bunting's Shadow'. Artists' ghosts brush past one another at Wylam station: where Bunting wrote his epic of disguarded love, Bolam travelled with her "teenage love," did her homework, as (perhaps) ideas for 'The Peepshow Girl' began. So "two shadows touched"; influences from each combining to produce new creations.

Islands, bridges, straits: writers find their inspiration in the liminal places. So it is with 'Solent Song'. The poet takes the gentle trip from Arran (as she explains in the notes) on the day the Scottish referendum was announced. The Solent saw the *Mary Rose* sink and *Titanic* depart; however calm the poet's journey, she knows these are dividing waters.

After a brief spell on land among foxes, cicadas, cave-dwellers, robins, we are back in water; or with those creatures most at home there. There is the "deepest-diving whale," its massive rising body the first sign of the Kaikoura earthquake and tsunami of 2016. Another whale, this one become an "old abandoned machine" is finally stripped down to a single arch:

"passed through by oblivious lovers
children who'd never seen the sea".

There is the Swedish sailor who sank with his ship in the 17th century, "preserved in mud" with his vessel, then raised and trapped above ground in a museum in the 20th. There is Robyn Bolam herself who, when reflecting on her own honeymoon cottage "pitched close to a wild cliff edge" realises the precarious state of her own fledgling marriage.

An alternative title for the whole collection could easily have been *Out of Their Element* – so many creatures act as unconscious fortune tellers caught between states or have a posthumous life in an alien environment. Bolam reassures us that there is strength in poise, but often we have no control over its resolution.

For me, ghosts have a stronger presence even than homes here: drowned boats' crews and writers' shadows of course, but also Bolam's memories of her mother's life as a nurse, her "cases…locked in her black bag". Maybe wolves still haunt the shoreline of Woolacombe after its surfers have gone home; certainly "raw light fizzes in the bloodless zoo" of the high voltage laboratory on the shortest night of the year. Indeed Robyn Bolam herself could be seen as having a second incarnation. Writing earlier under another name, her old one appears fleetingly as part of a respectful eulogy.

While the background notes she provides are useful, Bolam's work benefits from further research into the events and ideas behind the poems. You feel invigorated for having explored the depths, even while knowing you can never fully fathom them.

Tanya Parker Nightingale

Other anthologies and collections available from Stairwell Books

For further information please contact rose@stairwellbooks.com

www.stairwellbooks.co.uk
@stairwellbooks